# THE DAY HE ANSWERED

## Keeping The Testimony

By Krista Lesher

The Day He Answered
Keeping The Testimony.
Copyright © 2024 by Krista Lesher. All rights reserved.

---

No part of this publication may be reproduced, stored in a retrieval system or transmitted in any way by any means, electronic, mechanical, photocopy, recording or otherwise without the prior written permission of the author except as provided by USA copyright law.

ISBN: 9798878094498

Scripture quotations marked "niv" are taken from The Holy Bible: New International Version, Copyright © 1985, 1995, 2002, 2008 by Zondervan. Used by permission. All rights reserved.

Scripture quotations marked "nasb" are taken from The Holy Bible: New American Standard Bible, Copyright © 1995, 2020. Used by permission. All rights reserved.

Scripture quotations marked "nlt" are taken from The Holy Bible: New Living Translation, Copyright © 1996, 2004, 2007 by Tyndale House Foundation. Used by permission. All rights reserved.

Scripture quotations marked "nkjv" are taken from The Holy Bible: New King James Version, Copyright © 1982 by Thomas Nelson, Inc. Used by permission. All rights reserved.

Scripture quotations marked "tpt" are taken from The Passion Translation, Copyright © 2017, 2018 by BroadStreet Publishing Group, LLC. Used by permission. All rights reserved. ThePassionTranslation.com.

Scripture quotations marked "amp" are taken from The Holy Bible: The Amplified Bible, Copyright © 1954, 1958, 1962, 1964, 1965, 1987 by The Lockman Foundation. Used by permission. All rights reserved.

Cover design by Krista Lesher.

# DEDICATION

I dedicate this book to a special lady, Jean Groves, that we now call, "Mother of Revival." Even though she is now in Heaven with the Lord, I believe a large part of what has become known as the Summersville Outpouring is due to her faithfulness in prayer. Mrs. Groves prayed and believed for a genuine revival to come to our area for 60 years.

Many of us are walking in the answers of those prayers she prayed. We are experiencing the victories and claiming this land as our God-given inheritance, by uniting in prayer with the ones who have faithfully prayed and contended for revival long before our time. She, along with others, kept the flame of intercession burning. This is what it means to lean into the prayers of the saints. By leaning in, we align our prayers with the saints of old or cloud of witnesses. We purposely pray and agree with their prayers. We keep contending and walk-out what they started.

We had the privilege of tasting and seeing revival, even if only at a glimpse. This revival evolved from years of prayers. The Lord directed our prayers to come along side of the prayers she prayed. This union ignited a fire I will never forget.

I never had the privilege of meeting Momma Jean, as many call her, but I have heard the amazing stories from her daughter and spiritual granddaughter. As odd as it sounds, I get the feeling of having known her all along. I did have the opportunity to be a part of something amazing, though. Along with a few others, I had the most anointed worship nights I've experienced within her home.

What is even more amazing is the way it came about. The Evangelist, Nik Walker, who preached this revival, was invited to live in her house during the revival. This led to him living there for two years. We (his ministry team) would gather there to pray and worship the Lord. It was all God-ordained.

Momma Jean was led by the Lord to lay a foundation of prayer for revival. We received the honor and privilege of experiencing that revival. My good friend, Becky Keener (who you will hear me speak of in this book) is known as Momma Jean's spiritual granddaughter. We were talking once about Momma Jean, and I was sharing with Becky how much I wished I could have met her. Becky made the statement, "Oh Krista, she would have loved you!" I'll never forget how these words affected my heart. I knew then that the Lord had so much more in store for our small town. When the prayers of one saint can have such an impact, just imagine how much more our joined prayers can accomplish.

What are we yet to see? I ask this because, since then, I have met intercessors all over Appalachia crying out for revival. I know there are thousands more, like Momma Jean, who over the years have continued to pray and believe for a mighty revival. I believe we are going to see the greatest harvest of souls yet! Will you believe with us and pray?

**"So it shall be, when the Lord your God brings you into the land of which He swore to your fathers, to Abraham, Isaac, and Jacob, to give you large and beautiful cities which you did not build, houses full of all good things, which you did not fill, hewn-out wells which you did not dig, vineyards and olive trees which you did not plant—when you have eaten and are full—then beware, lest you forget the Lord who brought you**

**out of the land of Egypt, from the house of bondage".**

**Deuteronomy 6:10-11**

# ENDORSEMENTS

I want to thank Krista Lesher for documenting one of the greatest Outpourings I have seen in my lifetime. Sometimes the Lord puts people in our life that you can see that they have a genuine, wholehearted desire to please and follow Jesus. Krista is this kind of person. She has been a part of our family for over twenty years. I have had the privilege of watching her grow into one of the most anointed women of God that I know. I am thankful that the Lord allowed me to walk with her throughout the years, and see God move her from glory to glory. She truly has a hunger for God and His Kingdom. Her dream and desires were for a great move of God right here at home, and because of the God given dreams, we got to see a *seventy-day revival*. We got to see ETO become the Summersville

Outpouring, because Krista interceded, and believed God. Because Krista dared to dream and had Kingdom Vision, we saw churches come together and unite for the first time. We saw salvations, healings, baptisms, and a hunger for God in our community. We got to experience Kingdom connections that advance the Kingdom of God. All these things were made possible because we got to see... The Day the Lord Answered.

-Senior Pastor, Allen Travis
Restoration Fellowship Church


Many years of prayers for a true soul-saving, divine-healing, life-freeing Holy Ghost Revival came to us! I cannot express the gratitude I have for all those who yielded to The Lord by welcoming Him to invade our small town!

To some this may not mean much, but to us (especially Krista), it means everything! It means that God still answers! It means that as we put our faith in Him, He will not disappoint. It means that we can trust every Word He says. It means God cares, and He is faithful in all things.

As I reminisce on the days of the Summersville Outpouring Revival, my heart leaps with joy! I am forever thankful that Krista followed her heart and yielded to the Holy Spirit every step of the way. I longed for a Holy Ghost Revival, but had no idea when, where, or how it would come. To be honest, I questioned if I would see it. Little did I know, there were contenders and willing vessels, such as Krista, who were willing to go all the way! For that, I Praise The Lord and His Goodness!

As you read, "The Day He Answered: Keeping The Testimony," may your faith rise to new heights! That's what it does for me. The following pages raise my faith in remembering God answers! I am encouraged to expect more and to go all the way with God!

-Faith and More,

Becky Keener, Mountain Momma Rising

Author

# TABLE OF CONTENTS

Foreward……………………………………………14

Introduction………………………………………....19

Chapter1: Where Do I Begin?......................................23

Chapter 2: The Connection……………………….....39

Chapter 3: Almost Time……………………………..59

Chapter 4: So Much More…………………………...81

Chapter 5: The Personal Testimonies…………………97

Chapter 6: Lasting Fruit…………………………...135

Chapter 7: Maintaining The Fire……………….......151

Chapter 8: When It Doesn't Look Like What You

        Thought……………………………….......163

Conclusion………………………………………...183

# FOREWARD

In January of 2019, a pivotal prayer meeting in the mountains of Elkins changed the trajectory of my life and ministry. It was at this prayer meeting in the conference center of a small hotel that I accepted the position of the office of the evangelist in West Virginia. Of course, this was speaking prophetically of my call to full- time evangelism. At the time of the meeting, I was a youth pastor of a small church in Mullens, West Virginia. Almost exactly six months later, a conference began in Summersville, West Virginia that I was invited to speak at. The coordinator of this event was a woman that I was only vaguely familiar with, Krista Lesher. She invited me to the fifth year of her conference, ETO (Expect The Outpouring). My spirit was anticipating a great move of God. Little did I know that a revival of ten weeks would be birthed through this small conference that changed the lives of many people, including myself. It was at this revival that I fully stepped into the office of the evangelist.

Over the span of these ten weeks, I witnessed the miraculous take place. I watched entire football teams come straight from practice to church and give their hearts to the Lord. I witnessed people get out of their wheelchairs and push them out the door. We watched as nearly 350 people from several states received Jesus as their Savior. Still, almost 500 were baptized in the Holy Spirit with the evidence of speaking in tongues. A generation was set ablaze in a community that was longing for a true move of the Spirit. Seven churches came together for this revival, all of which were of different denominations. The fruit of this revival is still being birthed in the local churches of the area. Summersville and surrounding communities will never be the same.

As I reflect upon this monumental shift that took place, my heart is eternally grateful for the "yes" of Krista Lesher. She, too, was the youth pastor of the church hosting this conference. Yet, her "yes" extended far beyond the youth group. Her vision was completely set on the Kingdom of Heaven and seeing it come to this generation. "E.T.O" was more than a catchy phrase for a conference name. To Krista, it is her heart's cry. From this revival, Krista began to walk in a full- time capacity with Nik Walker Ministries, and she still serves today on my ministry's board of directors. She walks in the true anointing of "spiritual mother," and the title of mother goes beyond her own three children. Truly, she is mothering a generation. There will no longer be a day that I do not think of Krista as "mom." No one understands the sacrifice and travail that takes place before the birthing of a child quite like a mother. In the

Spirit, it is no different. This revival touched the hearts of many across Appalachia, but few will understand the sacrifice that it took to birth such an unprecedented level of awakening in a community. Many see and celebrate the fruit without realizing the toiling that it took to plant the seed in the ground. Although I was the minister of the revival, I am fully aware that the fruit does not belong to me. This tree is Krista's, and I am honored to have helped in the birthing of her vision.

For my spirit, this book serves as a reminder of the things that took place, but it is also the realization that without the obedience of Krista, I would not have been able to realize the fullness of the office I am called to walk in. Her faithfulness to the vision, even when it looked bleak, will be spoken of for generations. This book is the fruit of that faithfulness.

**"Behold, I am doing a new thing, now it will spring forth; will you not be aware of it? I will even make a**

roadway in the wilderness, Rivers in the desert." –

**Isaiah 43:19**

-Nik Walker

Evangelist and Author

# INTRODUCTION

July 19, 2019-September 28, 2019

70 Days

ETO-Expect The Outpouring became the

SUMMERSVILLE OUTPOURING

10 WEEK REVIVAL that began as a 3 Day Conference

Oh, what God can do…

The story I am about to tell is of an event that took place in Summersville, West Virginia. It is an event that many over the years had soaked in prayer and tarried for. It is an event that I pray will be talked about in years to come because of how it impacted hundreds of lives. It became a spark, a precursor, and the beginning of what the Lord birthed in the city of Mt. Nebo, West Virginia and became a resting place in Summersville, West Virginia. There was a Fire that fell upon this city that began July 19, 2019. A Fire that touched me, my entire church, and entire community. I, personally, would never be the same.

I knew the Lord wanted me to tell this story so things would never be forgotten about all the Lord did in this season. If He could do it for us, He could and would do it for others. This was the birthing ground of something bigger than us, bigger than our churches, and something bigger than our city. It was the heart of revival to spread across our state and throughout the land. It was the promises of God coming to pass right before our eyes that many could be won to the Kingdom. It was Jesus coming down and touching us right where we were, *Fire* falling upon us, tongues of fire resting upon us as is spoken in the book of Acts. It was the Holy Spirit manifesting right before us in signs, wonders, and miracles. This event that I am speaking of started as a three-day youth and young adult conference called ETO and later became known as the Summersville Outpouring!

I recently had a dream that I believe sets a precedence for this book and will help bring it all together.

Dream

I was sitting at a table in what seemed like a kitchen. At the table with me was a much older woman. I could not see her face, but I knew she was very special and her purpose for being there was of great importance. Also, at the table was one of my nieces who is in her teens and known to be a very sweet young lady. I was sitting at the table, in the middle, between the two. This table was a round table which stood out to me. The older woman grabbed my niece's hand as if imparting something to her as I was in the middle of them.

## Meaning

I believe the interpretation of this dream is a representation of three generations. The importance of the older generation and the younger generation coming together for such a time as this, is of great importance for the end of time harvest of souls we are about to see. We must be willing to tap into the prayers and wisdom of the older generation, unite it with the zeal and passion of the younger generation, and realize we all make up the Bride of Christ. I believe my generation is vital to help bridge the gap for the older and the younger to unite. We all have a job to do. Time is short, so the time is now to get busy. I believe the round table we were setting at was a representation of unity. I believe we are about to see this come full circle. Sit back and enjoy the read and realize that the Lord desires for you to encounter Him as never before.

# Chapter 1

# WHERE DO I BEGIN?

Where do I begin? I guess I could start with who I am and why I am writing this. My name is Krista Lesher, and I am from a small town in Fayette County, West Virginia. During this season, I was forty years old and married for twenty years with three young adult children. I attend Restoration Fellowship Church located in a small town called Mt. Nebo, West Virginia, in Nicholas County. At the time of this event, I was currently the young adult pastor at Restoration Fellowship also known as, RF Church, and had been for just over a year. I have attended our church for approximately twenty years. I was saved at nineteen years old and got very involved in the ministry at our church. I grew up in church my entire life and come from a heritage of pastors in my family. I must admit though, I was a joke at living this life throughout my childhood and teenage years. I was extremely rebellious and did a lot of damage to my own life. I ran from the Lord until He got ahold of me at nineteen. That alone is another story for another day. At nineteen, I truly encountered Jesus and He became more real to me than ever before. He radically transformed me! I now get the honor and privilege of telling you this story, which I do not take lightly in any way.

After three or four years of being involved with the church, I became Youth Pastor of the youth group. I had no clue what I was doing at the time, I was 22 years old. Little did I know I would end up being over the youth for the next 18 years. Crazy, right? I went through a lot of discipleship and training. I had a hunger to discover as much as I could. I had to try and do this well. Plus, I had a pastor who poured into me constantly. He taught me how to walk this thing out and supported me continuously, even when I got out of line. He is a true leader, one I learned from by his model and example.

It was in July of 2018; the Lord moved me from youth to young adults! I felt the Lord dealing with me for over a year to move in this direction. My heart was to see this generation living boldly for the Lord. I was tired of seeing young people graduate and then walk away from the Lord! Little did I know, this was the beginning of a transition the Lord was about to bring in my walk.

Let me back up a little! While over the youth group starting back in 2014, the Lord began to stir me for things I wanted to see Him do. We would always take our young people on trips, which I loved so very much. My heart has always been with this generation/youth and young adult age because of the life I had walked through during my years as a child, youth, and young adult. My heart burned for a generation! I desired to see greater things take place within them, and I was fed up with the enemy stealing a generation who carried purpose, passion, and zeal. I believed the Lord wanted to use this generation to spark something new within the church. On the search I went to dig a little deeper!

## ON THE SEARCH I WENT TO DIG A LITTLE DEEPER!

I remember it was always the same routine, we would take our young people to places like Winterfest in Tennessee, where we would join a crowd of young people of close to 20,000. We loved seeing how the Lord would use these trips to speak to our young people. Unfortunately, it seemed they would have an experience, be on fire for a little while, and then go back to their old lives. I was in search for something different and deeper. I remember a good friend of mine had told me about a free event called Warriorfest with Perry Stone. So, I was game, "Let's try it," I said. I was tired of the routine.

I will never forget the first year we went. There were only six of us, my two youngest children being two of the six. It was one of the greatest encounters! I say encounter because it was so different from what we had been used to. It was more intimate and real. It gave me a new hunger. We decided that this was the new place to bring our youth. Not only that, but the Lord began to birth something within me personally. He began to stir something deep within my heart. He began to stir my spirit for something. I could literally feel a birthing within me to cry out for our entire state and for this generation to be on fire within it. It became bigger than the four walls of our church. My vision was expanding.

I can remember as I was preparing and planning for our youth one day, I began to write in my journal things I desired to see take place.

Looking back now at the things I had written down; it almost overwhelms me to see how the Lord has been so faithful to bring them to pass. I am so humbled as I look back over all He would allow me to be a part of, in this time and season. All that we had witnessed and encountered through the Summersville Outpouring, the event this writing is focused around. I can look back now and say, "Don't despise small beginnings." I can also look now and see He was setting a plumb line in place to bring everything into alignment.

*"The hands of Zerubbabel have laid the foundations of this house, and his hands will finish it. Then you will know (recognize, understand fully) that the Lord of hosts*

*has sent me [as His messenger] to you. Who [with reason] despises the day of small things (beginnings)? For these seven [eyes] shall rejoice when they see the plumb line in the hand of Zerubbabel. They are the eyes of the Lord which roam throughout the earth."*

<u>*Zechariah 4:9-10 AMP*</u>

In my journal, it was in July 2014, I can remember writing down that I wanted to see a conference held in our state for youth and young adults. We had always taken our kids out of state for events like this to have a great encounter with the Lord. I began to ask, "WHY NOT HERE?" I can remember asking that question to the young people, "Why can't we have this here? Why could we not have something here within our state, within our city?" All it took was a vision and the feet to put it into action.

# ALL IT TOOK WAS A VISION AND THE FEET TO PUT IT INTO ACTION

The vision was born! I could not contain what I felt the Lord was stirring inside me. I desired to see a prophetic conference come forth that would draw young people. We even tried doing this a few years before but had to cancel it due to a sickness that attacked me, a sickness so severe that it caused me to have to step away from youth ministry for a short season. I knew it had been an attack from the enemy trying to get me to throw in the towel. I also see now that the Lord was preparing us and getting us in line for things to operate on His time, His agenda, and for His purpose.

I remember telling our pastor what my heart was longing for. I still remember where I was standing and where he was sitting as we discussed these things. Our Pastor, Allen Travis, a great man of God, was on board.

Still to this day, our pastor has always been for this generation. He has supported, led, and pushed us forward in everything we have put our hands to. I knew he believed in me and my heart for the Lord.

The preparation began! I remembered the Lord just giving me ideas of how to bring this together. I knew I did not want it to be the same as what we had seen before. I did not want routine, I did not want what was familiar, and I did not want what others had done. I wanted new and His Spirit in all of it. It began with a name. I wanted young people to encounter what I had been awakened to. The words "experience" and "encounter," kept coming to my heart. I remember one day seeing a vision of what this was to look like. I saw hands held out like a cup, and water pouring over them from Heaven. I remember explaining what I was seeing to my husband and asking him to draw it out for me. I still have a copy of the picture! This picture ended up being the first picture on our t-shirts we made. I knew it was "The Outpouring." Then the letters ETO began to be shown to me. I couldn't quite get the meaning, but I knew the Lord was showing me something. I began to write words on a piece of paper for what this may stand for.

*Then the Lord answered me and said,*

*"Write down the vision*

*And inscribe it clearly on tablets,*

*So that one who reads it may run.*

*For the vision is yet for the appointed time;*

*It hurries toward the goal and it will not fail.*

*Though it delays, wait for it;*

*For it will certainly come, it will not delay long.*

***Habakuk 2:2-3 NASB***

I can remember sitting and just staring at the paper asking the Lord what He wanted. I remember writing the word "experience," but I was never settled with just an experience. That was the whole thing I was trying to get away from. I wanted a real, genuine, authentic encounter, and I knew that the scripture in <u>Acts 2</u> and <u>Joel 2</u> were the visual of what we wanted to see take place. I wanted this scripture to come alive in a generation. I was so hungry to see it and see it in abundance.

***These men are not drunk, as you suppose. It's only nine in the morning! No, this is what was spoken by the prophet Joel:***

***"'In the last days, God says,***

***I will pour out my Spirit on all people.***

***Your sons and daughters will prophesy,***

***your young men will see visions,***

*your old men will dream dreams.*

*Even on my servants, both men and women,*

*I will pour out my Spirit in those days,*

*and they will prophesy.*

*I will show wonders in the heaven above*

*and signs on the earth below,*

*blood and fire and billows of smoke.*

*The sun will be turned to darkness*

*and the moon to blood*

*before the coming of the great and glorious day of the Lord.*

*And everyone who calls*

*on the name of the Lord will be saved.'*

<u>*Acts 2:15-21 NIV*</u>

*'And afterward,*

*I will pour out my Spirit on all people.*

*Your sons and daughters will prophesy,*

*your old men will dream dreams,*

*your young men will see visions.*

*Even on my servants, both men and women,*

*I will pour out my Spirit in those days.*

*I will show wonders in the heavens*

*and on the earth,*

*blood and fire and billows of smoke.*

*The sun will be turned to darkness*

*and the moon to blood*

*before the coming of the great and dreadful day of the*

*LORD.*

*And everyone who calls*

*on the name of the LORD will be saved;*

*for on Mount Zion and in Jerusalem*

*there will be deliverance,*

*as the LORD has said,*

*among the survivors*

*whom the LORD calls.*

<u>*Joel 2:28-32 NIV*</u>

This would be the place that God would pour His Spirit out on His sons and daughters. I was not going to settle for an experience. I wanted it to be our way of living! JESUS ENCOUNTERS that transformed EVERYTHING.

**I WANTED IT TO BE OUR WAY OF LIVING!**

Then the Lord spoke to me of expecting Him to show up. He was birthing something, so why not expect it to arrive. Therefore, ETO-Expect The Outpouring became pregnant within my spirit. I began to expect its arrival.

ETO-Expect The Outpouring is based on Acts 2:17-21. It became an annual conference geared to impact a generation to live out the Word in these last days. Jesus said, "Greater works we would do" (John 14:12). I was not going to waste any more time not doing what Jesus commanded us to do, which was to make disciples! When I say make disciples, I mean walking, talking, and doing exactly what Jesus did and more.

The last year of ETO was in 2019. It was truly the greatest ETO we have seen. From it, the Summersville Outpouring was born, which lasted for 10 straight weeks, 70 days in total. The very reason I am writing this story. To gain full understanding, I feel you need to know the beginning of the story. I believe the Lord has been bringing things into alignment for many years of what He wanted to do in the city of Summersville. This goes back even further than the first stages of ETO.

Why do I say this? Because of all the alignment we have seen take place and the people who have shown up along the way. I believe the Lord works in the details of everything, and we can see that throughout the Word of God. Sit back and hold on! My prayer is that you encounter His presence like never before. I pray you begin to see that the Lord cares about the details of your life, and He may be trying to align you with His will. Are you ready and willing?

***The steps of a good man are ordered by the Lord, and He delights in his way.***

***Psalms 37:23 NKJV***

# Chapter 2

# THE CONNECTIONS

A couple of years ago the Lord stirred my spirit to attend AD-SOM (Appalachian District School of Ministry) through the Assemblies of God. You are probably asking why this is important to our story. It goes back to the way the Lord orchestrates and aligns everything. I attended AD-SOM with a desire to learn more.

There was a lady at AD-SOM the Lord highlighted to me. She attended a church in Summersville, West Virginia, and I was familiar with her from some events that had taken place in the community. As the classes carried on, I found myself talking with her about different ministry events. I shared with her about ETO (Expect The Outpouring) and she shared about women's conferences with me. We were both event leaders. We kept in contact through social media and all the while, I knew there was something to our connection. Looking back, it was a true Kingdom connection. Little did I know that the Lord was drawing her to our church and aligning us for what was to come. Before I can carry on with this connection, I must tell you of another Kingdom connection that ties these together. Stay with me and don't lose me here.

In October 2018, there was an event called the Coalfield Awakening held in Beckley, West Virginia. This event was orchestrated by Nik Walker who is connected with Perry Stone. At the time, I was working for a Christian radio station, 106.9 Spirit FM located in Fayetteville, West Virginia. I learned of this event from a mutual friend and decided I would be bold and reach out to Nik Walker and ask him about visiting our radio station to get the word out about this event. I had a burning in my spirit to know more about this event that was coming to our area. I knew I did not come across The Coalfield Awakening by accident. I knew of Perry Stone and the ministry events he hosts. One event he does is "Warriorfest." This is where the Lord began to birth my personal hunger for more within our own state.

I reached out to Nik and was surprised at how quickly the connection between us was made. He responded almost immediately and agreed to come to our station and share about the event. We kept in contact after this and continued to plan a time for him to come. He set up an interview for us to have with Perry Stone as well. I'll never forget it, I was so excited to have this young man, Nik Walker, and Perry Stone on the radio! **I felt in my spirit like there was a shifting about to take place.** From the first moment Nik walked into the radio station, I immediately felt a God connection with him. There was no striving, no performance, just two Jesus freaks hungry to see a move of God!

I had previously heard about Nik Walker before the interview. West Virginia teachers were on strike in March 2018. I saw a video posted where this young youth pastor brought his youth group to the capital and prayed a powerful prayer for the teachers. It caught my attention, and I could not get it out of my mind. What stood out to me was the boldness he carried. Though I knew nothing about him, the Lord was highlighting him to me for a reason.

We took our youth to Warriorfest that same year which was at the beginning of April 2018. Perry Stone called forth this young man and spoke about how he had prayed for the teachers and confirmed that the Lord led him there. I was in awe with all I felt the Lord was showing me. Little did I know, He was setting things in place and working out the details as He always does.

**LITTLE DID I KNOW HE WAS SETTING THINGS IN PLACE AND WORKING OUT THE DETAILS AS HE ALWAYS DOES!!**

After realizing this was the same young man orchestrating the Coalfield Awakening, I knew there was something about him that the Lord wanted me to see. I couldn't quite put it all together, but the Lord kept bringing him to my attention.

As I was preparing for the fifth annual ETO Conference in 2019, I had not settled on who I should ask to speak that year. I always prepared for this conference early. I prayed continuously about who the Lord wanted to speak. I knew worship would be led by an amazing and anointed group of young people, "CVG." (Side note: If you have not heard of them, I encourage you to check them out. You will not be sorry.) CVG is a group of young people the Lord has raised up to help usher in the presence of the Lord through their heart for worship. I have been connected to them for several years and they have been a part of ETO in the past. God has used them in powerful ways. Little did we know that the former years of ETO were only the beginning of what the Lord had in store for the following weeks. I am so grateful for our connection and alignment the Lord orchestrated years in advance. CVG is very special to my heart, and I am forever grateful for their commitment in helping to usher in *Revival* that changed many for eternity. The Lord used these young people in such a powerful way and is continuing to do so to this day.

Back to the preparation. I had everything in line but still no speaker. I had asked one person, and they were in prayer about it. I had thoughts about another person, but still nothing. My mind kept going back to this young man, Nik Walker. I wondered if he would be a possibility. I questioned if I should ask. I had only heard him preach at the Coalfield Awakening and he only knew me as a radio show host. I wasn't sure, but I knew his name continued to come up. I remember sitting and talking with our Pastor and his wife in the sanctuary sharing my thoughts about the young man who kept coming to my mind. Our Pastor's wife said, "Just ask him!"

We were preparing for our annual youth trip to Warriorfest 2019. We got to Tennessee on March 29, 2019, for the first night of the event. Guess who we seen? Nik Walker with his youth group! The first night there the Lord moved so mightily, and our youth group was one of the last groups to leave. I saw Nik with other young people hanging out and praying for others. The Lord dealt with me about asking this young man to speak at our conference. I wanted to hear God clearly. You would think by this time

45

I would have had a clue that Jesus was setting it all up, but I was too busy being Gideon throwing out my fleece over and over again. Night two at Warriorfest and I was literally wrestling with myself. I was praying and just asking the Lord to please tell me when I was to ask Nik, and I heard Him say **"NOW!"** I questioned Him and asked the Lord, "You mean right now"? Again, I heard, **"NOW!"** Standing directly in front of me about 20 feet away was Nik Walker with his youth group. I got bold and decided I was going to walk up to him and ask if he remembered me from the radio station. I walked up and introduced myself, we hugged, chatted for a moment, and I told him it was good to see him again. Then, I just said it, "So we are having a youth and young adult conference this year called ETO, I was wondering if you might like to speak at it?" Before I could even get all the words out of my mouth, I heard him say, **"YES**, send me the dates!" I was stunned and could hardly believe it. Again, I must say the Lord was setting things in place and was going before us all. It was from that moment; I knew the Lord had his "**YES**" and things were going to be different this year.

**IT WAS FROM THAT MOMENT; I KNEW THE LORD HAD HIS "YES" AND THINGS WERE GOING TO BE DIFFERENT THIS YEAR!**

The Lord continued to stir my heart for ETO, and I knew in my spirit that something was really different about it that year. Every time I would get around our Pastor and his wife, they would tell me how excited they were for ETO 2019. I believe they were searching and needing something to happen. ETO continued to stir within me unlike any year before. That is the only way to explain it. There was just something different I was feeling.

## THERE WAS JUST SOMETHING DIFFERENT I WAS FEELING

Our church, Pastor, and his family had been through a hard season. Things were just weary and heavy. There was a sense of desperation, and we needed the Lord to move in a big way.

## THERE WAS A SENSE OF DESPERATION AND WE NEEDED THE LORD TO MOVE IN A BIG WAY!

The Lord had highlighted Isaiah 43 to me, and I continued in prayer asking for the Lord to do a new thing.

*For I am about to do a brand-new thing. See, I have already begun! Do you not see it? I will make a pathway through the wilderness for my people to come home. I will create rivers for them in the desert! The wild animals in the fields will thank me, the jackals and ostriches, too, for giving them water in the wilderness. Yes, I will make springs in the desert, so that my chosen people can be refreshed.*

*<u>Isaiah 43:19-21 NLT</u>*

As a church, we were in a dry place and needed refreshed. We prepared for ETO 2019, by working with the youth in dramas, skits, and by advertising the event. I kept in contact with Nik during this time and he continued to tell me himself that he had a feeling about this event. He told his team to pack extra clothes even though it was only a three-day event. I was hoping the Lord would do something supernatural, but I just wasn't sure of what was to come. I only knew my hopes were high. I felt an "expectancy" the Lord had birthed in my heart from the beginning of the ETO vision.

Little did I know, this moment was about to be the delivery of the vision the Lord had birthed years before. I can now see why our spirits were stirred and why we sensed something different was about to happen. This baby was coming forth and the time was now! I now understand why there were some complications and questioning in the delivery process that took place. If you know anything about pregnancy, there is a conception, a time of carrying the baby, and then labor and delivery. The Lord birthed the vision years before, in my heart. I carried it for a long season, then labor pains began. It was time to give birth to this vision.

As we continued to prepare, I became a little worried. I felt that no one was taking this seriously enough. I wondered many times if I was alone in my efforts to see this vision come to pass. None of the dramas were coming together and I couldn't get people to commit. I wondered if we were supposed to have dramas and could we be ready. I felt a complacency from so many around me. **I wondered if anyone wanted this as badly as I did.** I remember being in the church working and no one else around. I would just go and lay at the altar and ask the Lord to do something, whatever He wanted and to help me be obedient to His will. I would cry out in desperation!

I received messages from Nik, asking me questions about our people and if they were ready. I wondered about that myself. I knew what I was hoping for, and I knew our Pastor needed to see the Lord do something powerful as well. I begged God to do something special because I had saw a lot of hurtful things take place with my Pastor and his family. My heart was to see God move even if it was just for them to be refreshed. I knew it was possible, so I kept telling myself that.

During this time, our Pastor began preaching on prayer and the importance of prayer. He stated that the church would be called a House of Prayer and that we needed to return to that. We started having more prayer nights and some would come to pray, and the Lord began to use people to share what God was showing them. I believe this helped build on the foundation for what was about to take place.

**I BELIEVE THIS HELPED BUILD ON THE FOUNDATION FOR WHAT WAS ABOUT TO TAKE PLACE!**

Bringing it all together, remember the lady I mentioned at the beginning of this chapter? It so happened that she had a connection with Nik Walker as well. This lady started attending our church and so I talked to her more about ETO. The Lord grew my friendship with her. (Side note: Becky Keener and I are now very good friends. She and I are in ministry together. Becky had a vision from the Lord, and we now have Mountain Momma Rising ministry. I believe what the Lord ordained within ETO/Summersville Outpouring helped to merge our friendship together for the ministry that came later.)

I went to a prayer conference with Becky one weekend that was held at the Appalachia Prayer Center in Jesse, West Virginia. This center, which I did not know about at the time, was a Prayer and Revival Center led by Pastor Jay Morgan. Their purpose is to cultivate the flames of intercession and revival through strategic prayer gatherings and training in various parts of Appalachia. This event I attended with Becky was about a week prior to ETO 2019. This ended up being another Kingdom connection the Lord brought into my life. I will never forget it. I walked in and walking out of the sanctuary was Nik Walker. (Take note:

the Lord knew exactly what He was doing!) I ran up and hugged him. We were both blown away to see each other there and he proceeds to tell me the connection he has there with the Pastor of the church. That is the same connection Becky had as well. The Lord was connecting the dots all around me. **Do not ever take for granted the people the Lord aligns you with.** (Be discerning of course!) I guarantee it has purpose and it is always greater than what we can wrap our minds around. Those alignments should always have Kingdom purpose and not selfish agenda. That is how you know it is from the Lord, -**Kingdom purpose**!

    The day goes on and while I am at this service the Lord gives me a word for ETO 2019. I needed to hear from the Lord because I wasn't sure if we were ready or not. I remember being up at the altar in worship and prayer. I could feel the Lord begin to speak to me. I quickly went back to where we were sitting and grabbed my journal. This was the word the Lord spoke to me that night:

## JULY 11, 2019

*"I need you to be prepared for what I am bringing! Prepare your heart and your mind for what is to come! I Am the Lord your God and I will do what I have promised. I will bless those who are faithful. Trust in Me and do not fear. Trust in My Word. For I Am the Alpha and the Omega. I Am the Beginning and the End. I Am about to do something new."*

**(Isaiah 43:19 flooded my spirit once again!)**

The tears filled my eyes and here I am sitting in this large room full of people I didn't know. Yet, it felt like it was only the Lord and I were in the place. All I could do was begin to soak in the words I believed were straight from the mouth of the Lord. There was worship and praise, and a lot happening all around me at this service, but the Lord had swept me up in this moment. I was absorbed with Him and Him alone. I don't remember how long I sat in that moment, but it felt like forever. I can't tell you anything else that happened at that service. I only knew I was there for God's purpose and in His timing. The atmosphere at APC (Appalachia Prayer Center) made it possible for me to hear Jesus speak directly to me.

**(Side note: Don't dismiss the Lord when He comes and whispers to you. It's in those intimate moments that everything as you know it begins to shift. During those times, He is setting your mind and heart to be aligned with His will and His purpose even if no one else gets it, even if you, yourself, don't fully get it at that moment.)**

Now this was eight days away from ETO. It was interesting to me that we were eight days away because eight is the number for "New Beginnings!" I did not realize that until I began writing this. The Lord continues to blow my mind and piece together all the details.

Maybe you are reading this now and trying to understand all the connections and alignments that are taking place. I want to encourage you that the Lord does not make mistakes. He is perfect and is always about divine appointments. He knows what we need, when we need it, and even who to use in the process. He knows where you are right now, and He may be setting up that perfect alignment for your life. That person you need to minister to, speak into, or just bless specifically may be found in your path this week or in the days ahead. Be aware of your surroundings and look for the moments God may be highlighting to you. He may be birthing a dream inside of you this very moment that He desires to bring forth in time that will ultimately bring Him all the glory. He could be setting you (or whoever He places in front of you) up for Kingdom advancement that just may be "for such a time as this!"

**IT JUST MAY BE FOR SUCH A TIME AS THIS!**

# Chapter 3

# ALMOST TIME

July 13, 2019, I woke up from a dream that I knew had something to do with ETO. I knew there was something the Lord was trying to speak to me through it. The dream was a three-part dream, but I want to share only one of the parts at this moment.

<u>Dream Part 1</u>

*I was in a large room on a concrete floor. I saw what seemed to be a golden Labrador retriever dog laying on the floor. I quickly realized it was me and I was giving birth. I had 7 babies. There were 2 sets of triplets and 1 that looked a bit different from the others. My husband and I were in the dream, and we were holding the babies and washing their eyes. It was very vivid that the eyes were being washed out with soap and we were also trying to find names for the babies. All of these babies in my dream were boys.*

I remember waking up wondering what this all meant. I continued to dwell on it as the days counted down for ETO 2019. It reminded me of Mary and how she treasured these things in her heart.

**When the angels had gone away from them into heaven, the shepherds began saying to one another, "Let us go straight to Bethlehem then, and see this thing that has happened which the Lord has made known to us." So they came in a hurry and found their way to Mary and**

*Joseph, and the baby as He lay in the manger. When they had seen this, they made known the statement which had been told them about this Child. And all who heard it wondered at the things which were told them by the shepherds. But Mary treasured all these things, pondering them in her heart.*

<u>Luke 2:15-20 NASB</u>

This was when Jesus showed up on the scene in Bethlehem. Jesus was about to show up in our city. My hope is that as you read through this book you will ponder all these things in your heart. Allow the Lord to show up right where you are and realize He wants to come and make His dwelling among you.

*I felt the meaning of the dream was that the concrete floor represented a firm and solid foundation. The birthing of these babies was revival coming forth and the babies represented new life and vision. The washing of their eyes was for clear vision. My husband represented Christ, who allowed me to help in the washing of the eyes. A golden Labrador retriever represents, I believe loyalty, companionship, and friendship. The fact it was a retriever represented retrieving what the Lord was giving us and the color gold in the Bible was always prized and valued. Gold was brought to Jesus by the Magi, gold was refined and purified in the fire and was used in the construction of the temple.*

You may think it is strange about the dog in my dream, I did as well, but the Lord gave me this scripture.

**But she came and began to bow down before Him, saying, "Lord, help me!" Yet He answered and said, "It is not good to take the children's bread and throw it to the dogs." And she said, "Yes, Lord; but please help, for even**

*the dogs feed on the crumbs that fall from their masters' table." Then Jesus said to her, "O woman, your faith is great; it shall be done for you as you desire." And her daughter was healed at once.*

*Matthew 15:25-28 NASB*

I believe the Lord was about to give more than crumbs to His children. I will share more of this dream as we go. Two days later, the Lord spoke to me about "removing my hands." I had been given a word that I believe was from the Lord concerning this:

## July 15, 2019

"*Open your ears and listen Krista for I am doing a new thing as I have said before. Lead as I have gifted you but let your ears hear what the Spirit is saying. Do not lean on your own understanding. Acknowledge Me in all things and in all your ways. I will direct you each step of the way. Do not fear. Perfect love casts out all fear. Trust in my Word and in My Way. I have raised you up for such a time as this. Now trust the process and walk out the journey I have placed before you. I will do what I said I would do, but I need obedience. Be patient and wait on my timing, for My timing is always perfect. My ways are always higher. For I desire to give good gifts to My children, and I desire to pour My spirit out on those ready to receive what I have for them. For I Am a Faithful Friend, I Am loving, and I Am Righteous. I Am Alpha and Omega, I Am the Word made flesh, I Am with you always and I love my children."*

All I could do was weep at what I felt the Lord speaking to me! "Who am I that He would be mindful of me?" A good, good Father is who He is! I believe this word the Lord spoke also went along with my dream as well.

## THE DAY HAD ARRIVED!

July 19, 2019, the day had arrived!! I had been counting down the days and it was finally here. I was in a place of expectation but had some fear all at the same time. I remember getting up that morning and knew I needed some time with the Lord to hear His voice. I was setting at my kitchen table and had my Bible and journal out. I was in prayer asking the Lord to do whatever He wanted and to please show up and save. I felt the Lord begin to speak to me:

*"This is what I mean by removing your hands. You must remove your flesh. Get your flesh out of the way and be led by My Spirit. Your flesh will want to be in control but allow Me to do what I have come to do! Do not hinder, do not quench. Be in tune with my voice. Listen intently. My sheep know my voice. You have asked and I will answer. Are you not mine and do I not desire to give good gifts to my children? I AM who I say I AM!"*

The Lord reminded me of the scripture in the Old Testament in *2 Samuel 6:1-11*, which I encourage you to read that whole story. It is when David was bringing the Ark of God back into Jerusalem and it was placed on a new cart. Scripture says, "When they arrived at the threshing floor the oxen stumbled and Uzzah reached out to steady the Ark and the Lord became angry and struck him dead."

I knew what the Lord had to say was of utmost importance. I sure did not want to be like Uzzah and get in the way of anything the Lord wanted to do. The Lord continued to remind me of this scripture all throughout the revival and I continued to remind our leaders along the way as well. I knew if we did not allow the Presence of God, the Ark of God, to come in and fall wherever and however He desired we just might miss Him altogether. I had made up my mind that I would not be the cause of that, so when He said, "Remove your hands," I had to obey whatever it looked like. **I did not take this word lightly; I tucked it**

**in my back pocket and knew I needed to follow the Lord's lead.**

The countdown began and we were only a few hours away. I was nervous and excited all at the same time. Running to make sure all was in its place. I was hoping and praying for a great move of the Lord that I knew was so desperately needed.

The time came, the doors opened, and people were getting ready. I remember seeing Nik's prayer team prepping for the service. They were unlike any others I had seen before. They were in deep prayer and intercession in a room we had set aside for them before the service. Young adults crying out to God, praying in the Spirit, and asking for a great outpouring. It encouraged me and the presence in the building was already set. The anointing I witnessed these young people operating in, and the boldness they carried blew me away. This was not something they were flashing in front of people; this was what I witnessed them doing behind the scenes that stirred my spirit. I believe we were all hungry to see God do something that night and I could feel it about to happen in my spirit. I had shared earlier that I felt this year was different than any other in the past. Even in leading up to ETO. I knew things were going to be different, I just wasn't sure how. This baby was about to come forth.

**I KNEW THINGS WERE GOING TO BE DIFFERENT, I JUST WASN'T SURE HOW**

Worship began and we were carried straight into the Throne Room by the anointing of CVG. The Lord knew exactly what He was doing. He had put all the pieces in place for this night. We had set aside this moment to encounter Him and ENCOUNTERING HIM is exactly what we did.

## ENCOUNTERING HIM IS EXACTLY WHAT WE DID!

I will never forget this first night of ETO. It was like a wave of Glory came sweeping in the place. There was a great expectancy and a hunger for more. I wasn't sure of how everything would play out, but I knew Jesus was all I wanted in that moment.

## I KNEW JESUS WAS ALL I WANTED IN THAT MOMENT

The message preached that night from Nik was about the four soils. Looking back, I can see how the Lord was plowing up the ground in that place. The altar call came, and people flooded to the altar. People were crying out in repentance and laying on their faces. I was overwhelmed at what all the Holy Spirit was doing. It was in that moment I realized the Lord had so much more He wanted to do. I didn't know if we were ready, if I was ready, but what I did know is I was jumping in with both feet.

I was seeing my dream come forth through what was taking place during the altar call. People were being washed clean of their past and coming to a place of repentance. They were seeing with different eyes. People were hungry for Jesus and all He had to offer.

Recently, the Lord has been speaking to me about Ezekial 47. I love this chapter and all the detail within it. I could compare this moment of ETO to that scripture. What I mean by that is the water was flowing from the Temple and that was evident. We were encountering the outpouring! Yet, we had only reached ankle deep. The Lord wanted to take us deeper, and He still desires to do that. We have a choice of how deep we really want to go. I decided a long time ago that I refused to stay ankle deep! Like I said before, I was jumping all in. There is a depth that is limitless to the Holy Spirit and a relationship with Jesus. I am still searching out His mysteries. How about you?

## I REFUSED TO STAY ANKLE DEEP!

*Then he brought me back to the door of the house; and behold, water was flowing from under the threshold of the house toward the east, for the house faced east. And the water was flowing down from under, from the right side of the house, from south of the altar. And he brought me out by way of the north gate and led me around on the outside to the outer gate by way of the gate that faces east. And behold, water was trickling from the south side.*

*When the man went out toward the east with a line in his hand, he measured a thousand cubits, and he led me through the water, water reaching the ankles. Again he measured a thousand and led me through the water, water reaching the knees. Again, he measured a thousand and led me through the water, water reaching the loins. Again he measured a thousand; and it was a river that I could not ford, for the water had risen, enough water to swim in, a river that could not be forded. And he said to me, "Son of man, have you seen this?" Then he brought me back to the bank of the river. Now when I had returned, behold, on the bank of the river there were very many trees on the one side and on the other. Then he said to me, "These waters go out toward the eastern region and go down into the Arabah; then they go toward the sea, being made to flow into the sea, and the waters of the sea become fresh. "And it will come about that every living creature which swarms in every place where the river goes, will live.*

### *Ezekiel 47:1-9 NASB*

There is so much in these nine scriptures. I believe the Lord wants to flow through us. We are the temple; Jesus lives within us so the Holy Spirit should flow out of us. We tend to just look at the surface of things instead of digging deep into what Jesus really wants to say to us. It's more than a surface thing. It is a relationship that the Lord desires with us, to walk with us, talk with us, and speak the deep things of His Word to us. We cannot do this at a surface level. We have got to be willing to dive in and become immersed into the things of God. Then, it becomes who we are. Our walk and our talk changes. How we interact with one another changes. It becomes a love we cannot get enough of and a longing for more. The Lord is limitless!

*Then you will be empowered to discover what every holy one experiences—the great magnitude of the astonishing love of Christ in all its dimensions. How deeply intimate and far-reaching is his love! How enduring and inclusive it is! Endless love beyond measurement that transcends our understanding—this extravagant love pours into you until you are filled to overflowing with the fullness of **God!***

<u>*Ephesians 3:18-19 TPT*</u>

You cannot measure Him. We try to many times and try to fit God in our little box of what we think He should do or how He should do it, then we end up disappointed or offended because He didn't operate on our terms. He is God, not us! Last time I checked, it is God who sits on the Throne. We need to remove ourselves from the Throne, place the Lord back in control, and align things the way they are meant to be. I have had to reevaluate things in my life that I thought were right or how I wanted them to be. The Lord was clear to me that **alignment is key**. My heart must be aligned with the Lord's so that I may act, walk, and talk like my King. If I can begin to get this alignment correct, then I believe He will place the rest in order. That is what scripture says in *Matthew*.

> ***But seek first His kingdom and His righteousness; and all these things shall be added to you.***
>
> ***Matthew 6:33 NASB***

Let's look back to my dream. I believe the Lord was birthing something much bigger than all of us. I believe the Lord was operating in multiplication here, desiring to add to the Kingdom. The fact that there were two sets of triplets indicates the magnitude of what God wanted to do.

The one that looked different I believe was about becoming One Church. Seven is God's perfect number and the Lord is the Author and Perfecter of our faith according to *Hebrews*.

*Therefore, since we have so great a cloud of witnesses surrounding us, let us also lay aside every encumbrance, and the sin which so easily entangles us, and let us run with endurance the race that is set before us, <u>fixing our eyes on Jesus, the author and perfecter of faith,</u> who for the joy set before Him endured the cross, despising the shame, and has sat down at the right hand of the throne of God.*

<u>**Hebrews 12:1-2 NASB**</u>

The concrete floor represented a firm foundation, and the golden Labrador Retriever was about becoming loyal and a true friend. The fact it was golden represents a belonging to the Lord and purity. In <u>Haggai 2</u>, the Lord showed me so much prophetically, but specifically in ***<u>Haggai 2:8</u>***, ***<u>"The silver is Mine and the gold is Mine;" declares the Lord of hosts.</u>*** *"The latter glory of this house will be greater than the former,' says the Lord of hosts, 'and in this place I will give peace,' declares the Lord of hosts."* The washing of the baby's eyes was for the people to see in a brand-new way. It was a cleansing the Lord was doing. It was a picture of repentance. This is the key to Heaven! Jesus said in ***<u>Matthew 4:17</u>***, ***"Repent for the Kingdom of Heaven is at hand."*** My husband in the dream represented Jesus. Just knowing I played a part in aiding the washing of their eyes, humbles me to this day. I knew the Lord had heard the cry of my heart for years and the cries of saints who had gone on before us. One we know as the "Mother of Revival" Jean Groves. The Lord was adding to the Kingdom and people were laying themselves down and picking up their new identity. This was what I felt started to manifest the night ETO 2019 began! That seven-fold Spirit, the Spirit of God being manifested right before our eyes. I also want to remind you it was seven babies that were birthed from my dream. Could this represent the seven-fold Spirit we were about to see manifested before our very eyes?

*And I saw between the throne (with the four living creatures) and the elders a Lamb standing, as if slaughtered, having seven horns and seven eyes, which are the seven spirits of God sent out into all the earth. And He came and took the scroll out of the right hand of Him who sat on the throne. When He had taken the scroll, the four living creatures and the twenty-four elders fell down before the Lamb, each one holding a harp and golden bowls full of incense, which are the prayers of the saints. And they \*sang a new song, saying, "Worthy are You to take the scroll and to break its seals; for You were* *slaughtered, and You purchased people for God with Your blood from every tribe, language, people, and nation. You have made them into a kingdom and priests to our God, and they will reign upon the earth."*

<u>Revelations 5:6-10 NASB</u>

This is the reason why I cannot stay ankle deep. I crave for more of my King, the Lover of my soul, the One who rescued me when I was not worth rescuing. This is real love! How could anyone not want more of this? I continued the search for the depths of who He was as ETO pressed on. There was a far greater work taking place then what we could wrap our minds around. I was in great anticipation of what was to happen next. My question to you is, "What are you anticipating, or should I say who are you anticipating?" JESUS longs for you! He longs to wash your eyes clean to see as He sees. He longs to bring forth His will and His purpose in the earth, and desires to use you and I in this process.

**JESUS LONGS FOR YOU!**

# Chapter 4

# SO MUCH MORE

I am in tears as I am writing this to you. To look back at what the Lord done in that season is overwhelming. It is hard for my mind to stop racing and attempt to piece this all together. There was so much the Lord did, but He still isn't close to being finished.

We carried on as scheduled with the three-day conference, but the Lord was beginning to shake everything up. He was about to mess with our agenda of what we thought church should be like. I could feel everything around me was beginning to change.

# I COULD FEEL EVERYTHNG AROUND ME WAS BEGINNING TO CHANGE!

I can remember as we were preparing for night two of ETO, I wondered if we were to do our dramas as scheduled. These are the dramas I spoke of, that we were struggling to put together. I kept feeling like the Lord wanted to change everything. This is when the word He gave me came into play to "remove my hands." I pulled that word out of my back pocket and was holding it in my hand. In the middle of the service, I grabbed the mic and was ready to call up the drama team. I looked at Nik and even asked him if we should do the drama. He gave me a funny look, like why are you asking me. I will never forget this moment! The Lord was changing the service completely and I was trying to hear Him clearly. I did not want to miss Him!

We tend to get into a routine in church of how we think things should be done and who oversees doing them, and we program the Holy Spirit right out of our services. This is why we are not seeing *Revival* in our churches and living in a state of *Revival*. We put our hands on the Ark and try by our flesh to keep it from tipping over (2 Samuel 6). I knew something had to be different, at that specific time. The Lord was asking if I was going to follow what He was asking of me or, was I going to try and maintain everything to look good on the outside.

I decided right there; I was going with what I felt the Holy Spirit was leading me to do. We skipped the drama and went straight to the preaching. I removed us from ministering completely and allowed the Holy Spirit to have His way, as I got out of the way.

Many times, in our efforts to do ministry, we think we should be seen because of our anointing or because of what we can do. When the whole concept is to point people to

Jesus. I believe this was exactly what Jesus was trying to do in that moment. For us to have a real encounter and for our flesh to truly die!

The Word came forth and was preached with boldness and great conviction. Again, the altar was packed. There were more people that night as God was changing hearts and filling people with the Spirit. I couldn't believe it! We were seeing <u>Acts 2</u> and <u>Joel 2</u> come to life within our church and it was pouring out in abundance. It wasn't just one or two, but many that the Lord was moving on. You could hear people crying out for more of God, as they put everything else aside. They just wanted Jesus.

## THEY JUST WANTED JESUS!

What does it take to get to this place? I can remember the Lord replaying this scripture in my heart,

*Now to Him who is able to do far more abundantly beyond all that we ask or think, according to the power that works within us, to Him be the glory in the church and in Christ Jesus to all generations forever and ever. Amen.*

<u>*Ephesians 3:20-21 NASB*</u>

I can remember reading this scripture before ETO began. This helped spark my expectation, to see abundantly more than what I was even asking for. I was beginning to see it taking place before my eyes. I still wasn't even close to being prepared for what God was about to do next.

Souls were added to the Kingdom on night one and two of ETO. However, God was nowhere near finished! Night three arrived, and I was asking God for more of whatever He wanted. I began dealing with some opposition in a few areas, but I knew God was up to something. I couldn't let anything get in the way or allow what others expected of me, to hinder what Jesus was about to do. The program and order I had set up was completely thrown out the window and I knew many wouldn't understand that, but I had hoped that what we were experiencing would override self-will. Now this brings me to another part of my dream. Remember I told you it had three parts.

Dream Part 2

*The second part of my dream was a scene change. I was in a living room of a home of a lady I knew. The lady in my dream had a strong controlling spirit (which I had personally dealt with many times in real life) but in the dream she was speaking very negatively, degrading to me, and criticizing what I was doing. I can remember grabbing her by the neck, silencing the words that were coming from her, and cutting off and rebuking the things being said.*

I know this sounds very harsh, but as I stated before I was beginning to face a little bit of opposition on night two of the conference. I knew that the Lord wanted me to follow His lead. I could feel the shifting in my spirit and in the room, which I believe represented the scene change of my dream. I had people who were a part of the lineup that I did not want to disappoint, but the Lord was telling me to just follow Him. This was tough because I hate conflict if it can be avoided. Sometimes though in leadership you are faced with it many times due to the fact people don't always agree with decisions being made. I believe this is where the dream comes into play. I upset some people by not going through with the original plan, but I had to choke out the controlling spirit so it would not deter me from what I knew the Lord was requiring of me.

All along this was part of what the Lord was coming to do. It was for us to get on His page and His agenda. It was not what we thought church should be or how it should go, or even how it had been done in the past. He really was coming to do a "New Thing." I can look back now, and see He was disrupting everything, so His Glory could come in. This is why we may not be seeing the revival we are longing and praying for. When Jesus comes and steps on the scene, we want control of what He does so we don't get too uncomfortable. I believe this grieves the Holy Spirit. The Lord was continuously reminding me of the word He had spoken to "remove my hands" and let Him have His way.

**Prayer:**

**Oh God, help us that we will not grieve You when you so desire to come as You see fit and use who You desire to use. And let us not forget the times we cried out and asked You to do the very thing You want to do, even though it doesn't look like what we thought it would. Remove our flesh Lord and remove our hands from the grips of control.**

We began night three of the Conference and it was unlike any other! The presence of the Lord was so tangible in the place and the Lord began to operate with signs, wonders, and miracles. I'll never forget it, there was a lady who had one leg shorter than the other. She came forward for prayer and the Lord grew her leg out right in front of our eyes. That was just the start. A word of knowledge was given that someone there had scoliosis and needed healed. One of our own young people came forward who had dealt with scoliosis and pain for years. She was healed that night and her pain left. We put pictures of her back side by side on the screen for people to see the following night and the difference seen in her back was evident. By the end of the night, we knew the Lord was extending the three-day conference as a wave of *Revival* swept through. What was planned to be three days turned into ten weeks! Yes, you read that correctly, ten straight weeks of *Holy Ghost Revival*!

Every night built upon the next with salvations, people being filled with the Spirit, and physical healings. We arrived at day five of Revival. I remember being told that a young man who had been part of our youth group in years past, may show up to Revival due to what he had heard was happening. He had been dealing with cancer for about three years and was given a death sentence. I can remember how excited I was to know he may show up to Revival. I was hoping and praying to see it happen and believed for God to do a miracle. This young man was not just a part of my youth group from years past, but he was a very important part of our church and a part of my life. He was family to our pastor and his wife, and I was good friends with his mother. I had known these people for a long time, they were very close to me, and they were like family. Not only that, but I had seen this young man suffer so much, yet he had great faith through it all and was a true warrior in all he was walking through. I tell you this to make a point. He showed up on night five of the Revival. They had to wheel him into the church in a wheelchair and he was on oxygen. He was very weak and frail. I can remember my excitement and was asking the Lord to do something big. At the end of the service many people again were being delivered, set free, healed, and filled with the Spirit. Then what took everyone's attention was when this young man walked! He got up from his wheelchair and walked to the front of the room. He said he had no plan B, he was out of options, and he needed the Lord to move. Our church went crazy, and our faith increased. Hands were laid on him and people began to cry out, wail and shout to the Lord for his healing. I remember him walking across the platform and as he walked, he moved better and better and faster and faster. He stood upon that platform with his hands raised to the Lord. It was one of the most beautiful things I have ever seen. It was a sight to see! The entire crowd cried aloud and was praising God for what we were seeing take place. We all believed the Lord did something great that night and to this day I still believe that. This young man after that service, went on to marry the love of his life and go on a honeymoon that he was not capable of doing before or was even thought to be around for. I believe with all my heart; the Lord touched him specifically that night with hope and strengthened him to give him the desires of his heart and to extend his life to be able to do just that.

This young man went on to be with the Lord several months after revival ended, but he had been able to accomplish things that no one expected. He impacted more lives than we could ever count. I know his life and testimony continues to live to this day. The Lord has a way of doing something bigger than what we could think up on our own. Here is what I know! That fifth night struck something in this Revival and a true hope was released in our city. A hope to see the goodness of God be made manifest before our very eyes. Many may be saying, "But he wasn't healed," well I beg to differ. I believe the Lord did touch him supernaturally that night. He even testified about it on social media for all to see and believed himself, that the Lord touched him. How can we deny a personal testimony from the very source? I know what I seen that night and I know what I felt in the room. It sparked hope within him and those around him to give a fresh breath of air for this weary family to keep moving forward. This young man played a bigger part in this revival than anyone may ever say out loud. His faith alone helped fan the flame and set a tone for Jesus to do what only Jesus could do, in the coming weeks.

**The Lord has a way of doing something bigger than what we could think up on our own. Here is what I know! That fifth night struck something in this Revival**

**and fanned the flame to do what only Jesus could do in the coming weeks.**

I still believe the scripture that says,

*And we know that God causes all things to work together for good to those who love God, to those who are called according to His purpose.*

<u>*Romans 8:28*</u>

I often wondered if having experienced revival the way we did, was a way to help with the loss of this young man in our community and our church body. I don't know exactly, but what I do know, is that a fresh wind blew in with this revival and resurrection life was breathed back into dry bones. We would never be the same, or at least I knew for a fact that I never would be.

**WE WOULD NEVER BE THE SAME, OR AT LEAST I KNEW FOR A FACT THAT I NEVER WOULD BE.**

# Chapter 5

# THE PERSONAL TESTIMONIES

I have only shared a few of the testimonies throughout the beginning of this, but there were so many more. This will still be only a few, but to hear from people personally is the very testimony of Jesus. The Lord began to deal with me a few days into the *Revival* that I needed to document what was happening. I knew there needed to be a remembrance of all Jesus was doing.

I have gotten permission from these people to share their personal encounters and what the Lord did during this revival. I believe it is of great importance to incorporate their stories into this book, because the testimony of Jesus is the spirit of prophecy.

> *And I fell at his feet to worship him. But he said to me, "See that you do not do that! I am your fellow servant, and of your brethren who have the testimony of Jesus. Worship God! For the testimony of Jesus is the spirit of prophecy."*
>
> **_Revelations 19:10 NKJV_**

I recently read a book by Bill Johnson that spoke of this very thing and the importance of remembering. All throughout scripture we read of the Israelites and how they continued to fall into idolatry and sin, and the Lord would burn with anger toward them because they would forget constantly all Jesus had done for them. Every time, He would rescue and revive them. Then they would turn around and forget all He had done and fall into the same thing again and again and again. I don't know about you, but personally, I'm so tired of that. Is there anything we can learn from the scriptures here and put into practice for today, to help us remain on the straight and narrow, keeping us abiding in His Presence? I pray the answer is YES!! I believe if we would grasp this concept of "Remembering", we can grab hold of the testimony of Jesus, being the spirit of prophecy, and see Jesus and His Word come alive in our churches, in our cities, our counties, in our state, and then in our nation. Could learning this and walking it out, cause us to be in a state of Revival and therefore living revived?

Wasn't it Jesus Himself that said, "Do this in Remembrance of Me." (1 Corinthians 11:23-26). This speaks of Communion where we eat of the bread and drink of the cup to remember the sacrifice Jesus paid for our redemption. It wasn't just our redemption alone, there is much more that comes along with this. Jesus going to the Cross reconciled us to the Father; not only did He pay for our sin, but for our healing, our deliverance, and our complete freedom. Jesus died and rose again for all of this. Therefore, the very signs, wonders, and miracles we testify about in the Book of Acts are still in operation today. Jesus gave us access to all of this by the shedding of His Blood on Calvary.

These very signs, wonders, and miracles are exactly what we began to witness and encounter during the Summersville Outpouring. This ten weeklong Revival where the Glory of the Lord truly came and rested on our city. I refuse to allow this to just be another revival that is chalked up to a lot of hype and talk. I personally prayed for years for something like this to happen in our church, in our city, and in our generation. I, along with many other intercessors prayed for this, He answered, and many of us got to witness it firsthand. How can I not share all that Jesus did, not only for me personally, but hundreds of others?

For the remainder of this chapter my goal is to stir your heart and that faith would arise within you as you read personal encounters and testimonies from other people who attended the Summersville Outpouring and were impacted by it.

**Cynthiea Williams Testimony**

Even though time has passed since the Summersville Outpouring, I remember it like it was yesterday. It radically changed my life with lasting fruit. I had only been a true believer for about a year. I did not grow up in church, so I was very hesitant of most church activities. I wasn't interested in speaking in tongues, laying on of hands, fellowship, or worship. I wasn't against those things; they were not for me. That is until a friend invited me to the Summersville Outpouring and now my life is forever changed.

I had never experienced true worship or the Holy Spirit until then. It had completely wrecked me and changed my entire world for the better. I knew then God had so much more for me and wanted my full yes. I was a believer, but not fully committed to His will. When I said yes, everything changed. I began speaking in tongues, having visions and dreams, discernment of spirits, and words of knowledge.

During those weeks, the Holy Spirit was removing junk from me. Each night, God would break me down and put me back together. Removing anger, hate, bitterness, unforgiveness, sinfulness, and adding in righteousness, love, compassion, and forgiveness. He completely changed me. My thinking and actions were transformed. Prayer and fasting became a priority in my life. I could not get enough of the Word, worship, or prayer. My spirit craved more and still does.

Not only was my thinking and actions transformed, but also my body. I had been suffering with headaches daily for a while, but never had it checked out. Frankly, I didn't want to know due to my health history. One night while receiving prayer, I was overwhelmed by the Spirit, I fell, and hit my head. As I laid there, I heard in the spirit, "Your headaches are healed." I have not had one since.

Another miraculous healing that came forth for me was recovery from a stroke. I had not been feeling well, but I wasn't going to allow that to stop me from going to revival. As I was worshipping and praying, I started having a stroke. I typically only had mini strokes, but this was a full-on stroke. Left side of my body completely worthless, couldn't talk, think, or respond. Then everything went dark.

I was floating off to Heaven, it was so peaceful and glorious. I knew I was surrounded by praying people, I could hear them, but I was getting farther way. Then, I heard someone call my name, and it began to get closer and closer until I was fully awake. They continued to pray, and all symptoms of the stroke went away without any medical intervention.

When the Summersville Outpouring was ending, I was sad because all these churches that had come together as one would now go their own ways. But to me these people felt like family even though I didn't know them. We had gone through so much together during those weeks. Only we didn't know that God had a plan for those Kingdom connections in which He built during those weeks. I am lasting fruit of the Summersville Outpouring, forever changed, and forever grateful to those who were willing and obedient to Gods call to pray and fast for the everlasting fruit which many now bear.

## L.W. Testimony

He was 8 years old during the Summersville Outpouring and had a heart for true worship. He loved the Lord and trusted Him fully. He "HAD" cystic fibrosis which is a genetic disease that causes a lot of mucus build up in the body. Due to this, he fought many lung infections, stayed at poor health, and took a lot of medications. He was not growing well as his health declined.

The second week into revival, he went up to the altar for prayer on his own and it was the start of his healing. We held on tight and declared his healing daily. The following days he became under attack and his health got worse, but we serve a mighty God. His lung function declined, and his immune system was failing and could no longer fight off infections. But we kept declaring his healing.

As the revival continued, He grew closer and closer to the Lord. Always praying and worshipping, holding tight that he was healed no matter what the reports said. At the end of the revival, an altar call was done for those who needed healing. So, he went up again for prayer. Those who were praying for him, didn't just pray for a minute or two, but twenty. When they lowered him to the floor, he was speaking in tongues. Once he was able to get up, he was breathing differently. He said, "God spoke to me mom, He said I was healed." From that day on, he has been cystic fibrosis medication free. He is growing well and healthy. Lung functions are back to normal, lung damage reversed, and immune system working as it was intended to. Six months after revival, they even declassified his cystic fibrosis diagnose.

Side note from the author:

I remember one day in a Sunday Service this young man and his family came to visit our church during the midst of all the revival services. During worship, I seen this little boy come up front without a care in the world. He bowed down on the floor in a posture of worship and humbleness before the Lord. The image of this is still imprinted in my mind and I still talk about it with his mother. I didn't put it together and realize until later who this little boy was. He was the one the Lord had touched so radically. His heart for worship embodied true intimacy. This kid was 8 years old and understood what it really meant to worship the Lord and was demonstrating it out loud unashamed. It burdens me that most adults can't stay awake long enough for even one song during worship, or they set like a knot on a log because they just want things to move on quickly. We have lost touch with our entire purpose on this earth and that is to bring the Lord glory and worship Him and Him alone. Oh, how we need a heart like this young man, to have a true childlike faith.

## Karlee Moore Testimony

There are many things I could mention about this revival that changed my life. I could tell you about the lifelong friendships that has been made. I can tell you of receiving the gift of tongues. I can tell you of the new beginnings. Even of the many nights I seen healings and restoration. Even those that would bind together in unity. But for me it's the lasting fruits. I am a lasting fruit that has found herself. I learned that God would use whoever He needs to use in that moment. That all the years of me saying, "God what about my time," turned into selflessness and praying for their time. I learned that I am being used; even if it's not on a platform, but in the secret place with The Most High God. I found being a child of The King is greater than my gifts and callings.

This revival did more than heal our bodies but healed our souls. It made such a deep impact in the lives of many. In so much, that years down the road we are even more on fire for God. We are forever searching for a deeper connection and a greater revelation of our Redeemer.

**Aaron Moore Testimony**

There are many things I could testify about that happened during the Summersville Outpouring. I could tell you how I saw God heal people, from legs growing out, and Stage 4 cancer being removed from bodies. I could tell you how I saw God break the chains of depression, anxiety, heartache, and unworthiness. I could also tell you a story of how a Pastor from a little church had to make the decision to conform to the status quo of that church or chase the Glory of God. I'm not going to though; what I'm about to tell you defies explanation, it can only be categorized as a gift from God.

One of the many nights of the Outpouring, as it has become to be called, I went with my wife to experience what God had for us that evening. I remember during worship, Nik, the evangelist, had stepped out of the normal routine and was praying with people. When he came to me, I remember lifting my hands to receive, and Nik said to me, "The Lord wants to increase your discernment." The next thing I knew I was out on the floor. As I was laying there just basking in the presence of God, I was taken into a vision. I saw Jesus, what I could only describe as the typical Jesus that we have all seen in pictures growing up, and he said, "Follow me." As I got up it felt like my spirit left my body, and I walked beside Him to the back doors of the gym. As we walked through the doors, we weren't in the parking lot, instead we were on the roof of the gym. Jesus turned and said to me, "Do you want to see things like I do?" When the Lord asks a question like that are you really going to say no? So, I answered, "Yes Lord." Then He said, "Look out at the houses around us." As I did, I saw people inside their houses, but it was only a silhouette of them.  They were radiating light.  Some white, some gray, others black.  I didn't really understand what I was seeing.  The Lord then said, "The color of the light represents the person's relationship with me."  In amazement I began to look around the city of Summersville, white, black, and gray dots were everywhere.  Then it seemed like my spirit sank through the floor and was going back into my body.  As it was though, I saw a black dot going to the altar.  The closer it got the lighter it became.  Black, to gray, then white; the brightest white I ever had seen.  Later I found out that the dot I had seen was a Jehovah Witness coming to the Lord for salvation.  Many may read this, hear this story, and try to claim that it wasn't real.  Many have tried to claim that the Summersville Outpouring was an over-spiritualized, hyper-emotional meeting.  They have their own opinion, but I know for a fact, you can take it to the bank, this was a move of God Almighty, and no one can tell me different.  After everything that I have experienced, you can't convince me otherwise. If I had to leave you with something, it would be this. Serving God is exciting, and there's more to this walk with Him than we think there is. Chase after Him and the deeper things He has for you. You may even have to make a choice to go against the status quo of your church you are pastoring! I know I did, and because I did God has opened my eyes and mind to a much more intimate walk with Him.

**Lilly Meadows Testimony (Excerpt from Lilly's Journal)**

Night three of ETO, there was an altar call, and I went forward. I began speaking in the Spirit of the Lord and as I was praying, Brooke, a girl from Nik's prayer team began to pray for me and I began to fall out in the Spirit. I felt this burning sharp pain in my back. I didn't really think anything of it, I just figured my back was just hurting like normal. Then I began to get up and I was talking to my friend, and I heard the Evangelist Nik Walker say, "God is telling me there is someone in this room that has scoliosis and God wants to heal you, so please come up and let me pray over you." I started crying as everyone started praying for me and I could slowly feel the pain go away. I then went out in the Spirit again and as soon as I hit the ground, I felt all the pain go away and I have never been so joyful. I kept on feeling my back just as a reminder of how awesome my God is.

**Brooke Hall Testimony**

During the Summersville Outpouring, I can think of countless works that the Lord did in me. The most memorable one for me, however, was about three weeks into the revival where the Lord worked an inner healing in me. There was an elderly lady in a wheelchair, and a few of the girls on our prayer team had been praying for her. I walked over to join them, and I placed my hand on the woman's shoulder. I had my eyes closed, but I felt her gently grab my hand and begin to hold it. I opened my eyes, and she was already looking at me. She didn't say anything at all, she just looked at me and smiled. As soon as I locked eyes with her, I felt the Lord begin to shift something in my heart, as if every wall I had built up was shattering. In the previous years, I had become so numb to emotions due to hurt and other circumstances I had to walk through. I had a very hard time feeling, and my heart was hard. But in the moment that lady held my hand, and looked at me, the Lord began changing me. I suddenly became overwhelmed with compassion, and my heart felt like it was going to burst. Finally, I broke, but it was in the best way possible. I began weeping, and instantly I began feeling emotions that I hadn't felt in years. Everything that

I had become numb to was restored. I felt the Lord heal my heart and my mind. I felt Him restoring the broken parts of me, and I haven't been the same ever since. He restored my heart.

## Michael and Elizabeth Fagan Testimony

My wife and I have been married 10 years as of October 29, 2021. For eight of those years, my wife and I have tried to conceive a child, but it just would not happen. We had (I quit counting at) 13 miscarriages over that period of time. We wanted a baby so bad. We prayed fervently, we asked God, we begged God at times, but it just was not in his timing yet. We went to doctors in Harrison County, West Virginia, to find out what was wrong with us and why my wife's body kept miscarrying so early after conception. We were told we would never be able to conceive a baby without the help of medical science and doctors, that it had something to do with our blood types not being compatible and my wife's body rejecting my DNA.

We are not the kind of Christians who take no for an answer when there is an impossibility in our own understanding, yet; is perfectly possible in the hands of Jesus. We kept praying without ceasing.

Early 2019, I ended up in the intensive care unit for pancreatic complications. My A1C was at 14.1, that's beyond dangerously high. My triglyceride levels were off the charts, and I was in stage 3 hypertension. I walked into the hospital myself, and soon spoke to a doctor who was astounded I was conscious and speaking. They took me away to the intensive care unit, and while away, the doctor told my wife that she doesn't expect me to live and handed her last will and testament papers that she needed to sign. My wife refused and started praying. I spent over a week in the hospital and was diagnosed with type 2 diabetes. I was taking five shots of insulin a day and could not eat anything with carbs or sugar in it or my levels would skyrocket.

We got invited to a revival in mid-2019 in Summersville that was supposed to last three nights but lasted over forty. Just a little bit of background of my wife and I; we both believe in the healing power of Jesus. We both believe in the power of His Name, His Birth, Life, Death, Resurrection, and that He still lives today. We believe in the Holy Spirit and the gifts associated with the Holy Spirit. I am well aware of the power in faith, and how through faith in Jesus, miracles occur. In those 40 plus days, the Holy Spirit fell upon the city of Summersville and began to work miracles. People came from other counties, and soon other states.

At the beginning of this revival, God spoke to me, and He told me that He required something from me, and that I would have to willingly give up parts of me in order for Him to work in my life. Things I thought I had already taken care of, but I hadn't. So, in worship, I gave myself to God to let Him tear me down, to search my soul of anything unworthy, and I let Him change me. **Sometimes, when God wants to work in our lives, we hold Him back. We like to be in control instead of letting Him reveal Himself in us.**

Later in the revival, my wife and I received prayer three times from three different individuals, and God spoke to me again and told me, "You will have your son." I also prayed for healing from diabetes. I went from five shots of insulin helping me level my sugar, to zero shots a day, and my sugar was regulating by itself between 90 and 100. Highest it got was 110, but that's because I decided to eat ice cream to test it out, and it went back down to the 90's by itself. I was no longer on insulin but continued to test my sugar so that I could show my doctor if asked.

A couple of months later, my wife woke me up in the middle of the night screaming and crying. I thought there was an emergency, maybe someone broke in, or anything that could go wrong. I immediately reached for a .44 mag revolver I had hid at my side, due to just recently having a drive by shooting a week prior. I jumped out of my bed, and I was met by my wife, who was holding a positive pregnancy test. I was confused at first. She hands it to me, and I say "yeah... that's a positive," not knowing what else to say after being woken up in such a manner. We scheduled our first appointment, and of course they want a positive blood test from a doctor. We schedule it and it was positive. We had our appointment, and the ultrasound tech shows us this heartbeat about the size of the end of a pen. IT'S STRONG! We were overjoyed, and we start telling everyone. We were met with the question "Do you want to have a boy or a girl?" As a man of faith, I have to announce what God told me. I replied, "It's a boy, God told me my baby is a boy." My friends didn't have the same belief I did, so they were skeptical of my claim, but I kept insisting I knew the sex of my baby, according to Gods words to me. Other things were said too, like, "Maybe you should wait to see what the baby is before you get anything or pick out names." My brother-in-law, who is against God, insisted he was a girl, but I kept announcing by faith his gender.

This is the best part, the names. My wife had his name picked out early and had her mind made up, his name was to be Aaron Wyatt, but God had other plans. She was going through names and the name Simon just kept sticking out to her and she couldn't shake it. So, she changed his first name to Simon. I was looking at names, just to be looking, and I saw a name and God spoke to me and said that one. God chose the name Azariah, so we listened and changed his middle name to Azariah. These are both Hebrew names, and Hebrew names have biblical meanings.

*Simon meaning, "God has heard"*

*Azariah meaning, "God has helped"*

## "GOD HAS HEARD, AND GOD HAS HELPED."

Simon was born April 24, 2020, without any complications during pregnancy. When it came time to deliver, my wife could not dilate past .5cm. She was given drugs to force her to dilate. She was in contractions for three days, and still would not dilate passed a .5cm. Another doctor on her OBGYN team entered the room and said my wife had not had an ultrasound since Covid had begun, and they needed to get one. Come to find out, Simon's head was too big to fit through the birth canal, and he was folded like a futon mattress. A cesarean was the only way he was coming out, or Simon would die of suffocation. There is no other reasoning as to why my wife would not dilate while being on some serious drugs, other than God knew what was going on and forced her uterus to stay closed. I was blessed to witness a full cesarean, having had permission from the doctor of course. Simon came out blue and was not breathing at first. God had his hand on those nurses and doctors that day and he soon started breathing. He had complications at first with his sugar and oxygen levels. He pulled himself out of it within a couple of hours, and he was soon stabilized.

I'm quite confident that Satan was trying his hardest that day, but I'm more than confident in the power of my God.

### GOD PREVAILED!!

As you can see and hear from real testimonies, this is only a few things Jesus done, yet so powerful and life transforming. There were so many other healings that took place during this 10-week revival. It is hard to record them all, but I could mention just a few more. Like how a lady who had been in a wheelchair for over 20 years stood to her feet one night, or how a former Jehovah Witness came forward around night 29 during worship and surrendered her life to Jesus. Her words were, "I'm Free." We saw addicts come forward and surrender their lives to Jesus, true deliverance took place. People were driving from all over just to get in His Presence. Another favorite is when an entire football team showed up and surrendered to Jesus. They ended up canceling their practice and even went as far as announcing it on social media about the revival and their heart to support what the Lord was doing. They came back again, and the Lord touched the coach. We got to witness the players laying hands on others and praying. That is real revival!

This revival began within our church and grew to where we had to move it into a large gym; to hold all the people. People were coming from all around to get to this revival and encounter Jesus for themselves. This is where many of these testimonies you have heard came from. We were blessed to have seven or more different churches involved that caused this revival to thrive.

I pray your faith is stirred up and you realize that the Lord shows no partiality and desires for you to experience Him just as these people did. (Acts 10:34-48)

I want to end this chapter with one last testimony and that testimony is my own. I pray as all these others did, that my testimony will be a stirring of your faith as I continue to testify of Jesus and His undeniable goodness.

Like I spoke of before, I had been in much prayer for years asking the Lord to bring awakening to our youth and our generation. I desired for the Lord to do something specific within our church, but also to the entire community. I began holding prayer nights and encouraging our youth to come and pray and seek the Lord. Sometimes I would hold these on Saturday mornings or Friday nights. I opened it for anyone willing to come and meet with me and pray. Now, I must admit, I didn't have a whole lot of people that showed up. I think the very first one, it was me alone on a Saturday morning. But I was determined if it was just me, I would keep seeking. Sometimes only one or two other people would show up and pray for a little while. Some of the Prayer nights, which was called Fire Nights, I began having a few youth to show up. We were beginning to encounter the Lord in these Fire Nights and the youth would pray over one another and Jesus would minister and encounter us right there. As time went on though people began to dwindle out again due to conflicting schedules and school sports. Many times, it was just me praying and asking the Lord, "What was it going to take?"

## "WHAT WAS IT GOING TO TAKE?"

I can remember I had a specific place at the altar of the sanctuary I would lay on my face and bear my heart before the Lord. I would just cry out and ask Him to come and meet us, and that we were desperate. I thought by now I would have worn a place in the carpet. Please know that I don't share any of this to boast in anyway. What I am sharing with you is the hunger inside of me I carried and regular church and mediocre was not satisfying it. I knew there was more to Jesus. I had read about Him and His power constantly and I desired to experience what the men and women we talk about in scripture encountered. I knew it was still available for us.

I had a good friend, she and I were both intercessors, and we would talk about the things of the Lord and our hunger for more. It was a few years before the first year of ETO in 2015. We felt pressed to pray for our area. So, we took a week and drove to specific areas we felt led to go to and pray. There were three specific places that we went, we staked the ground, and we claimed revival over our land. The first place I remember going was the county line between Fayette and Nicholas County, West Virginia. We pulled off on the side of the road, staked the ground, and prayed. I specifically remember my daughter being in the vehicle with us and getting to witness and be a part of what we were doing. Another place we went was the New River Gorge Bridge. We staked the ground as we were overlooking the Gorge and began to pray and prophesy over our area. It was so powerful. The third place we went was Summersville Lake at the Dam. This one will forever stand out in my heart and mind. My daughter was with us this day as well. When we stopped at the Dam, I remember standing and looking out over the Dam and praying. All of the sudden we saw an Eagle flying as we looked throughout. It swooped down and had a snake in its claws as it was flying up higher. We were so taken back and in amazement at what the Lord was allowing us to see. We knew in that moment the Lord was marking us and that moment for what was to come. I knew this was truly a prophetic moment and I needed to write it down.

I share all of this because I believe what we did during this time was very significant. This played a huge part in seeing Revival come to our city in Nicholas County and it also tied our counties together. I also did not realize, at the time, that there were many other intercessors carrying the same vision and passion in their hearts as well, and they were crying out for Revival to come in our area. The Lord was taking account of our intercession and was hearing the cries of each of our hearts. I know that all these intercessors carry their own testimonies and stories, and each play a part of the bigger picture.

I could share so much and continue to testify of His goodness, but this book would not contain it all because the God we serve is limitless. I do believe the Lord sets up, aligns, and is strategic. Another example is when I was youth pastoring, I was eager to reach out and get people connected. I got connected with the Youth Pastor at the church down the road and we began to meet once a month taking turns at her church and my church to meet for prayer. We prayed for each other and prayed for our generation. We would cry out for Revival to come and bust loose over our young people. What is so cool about this, is the church she was a part of ended up being one of the main churches that connected with us when Revival broke out in July 2019. I believe our meeting together and praying was another part in stirring the embers for this Fire to ignite and to come forth. This church, my youth pastor friend attended, held a Prayer Meeting where I was told a well broke open during a powerful night of intercession and calling forth, just months before Revival broke out.

Sometimes we have no idea what all the Lord is doing until after the fact. As we look back and see how He specifically sets it all up, every detail for HIS GLORY. NOTHING IS WASTED!

**NOTHING IS WASTED!**

I must share these moments and testify of the Lord's Goodness because I know and believe that nothing comes forth without prayer and intercession. I have learned that over the years! Intercession is what I believe birthed this entire book to be able to be written. There is a thread all throughout this story and it comes back to intercession. We downplay intercession but do we realize the Greatest Intercessor there is, sets at the right hand of the Father and intercedes for us? To me that says intercession is of great importance!

*Who is he who condemns? It is Christ who died, and furthermore is also risen, who is even at the right hand of God, who also makes intercession for us.*

<u>**Romans 8:34 NKJV**</u>

All of this is a testimony of Jesus, of how He alone can set up, ordain, answer prayer, and hear us as we pray.

One more thing; not only did Jesus answer my prayer along with so many others, but He healed my body. During revival the Lord totally healed me. I had been suffering from chronic migraines that were so bad they would put me in bed for days. I also was on medication for these migraines and for seizures as well that the enemy attacked me with ten years prior to Revival. It was during this Revival the Lord completely healed me. I am no longer on any medication at all or suffer from any of these symptoms or illnesses. Don't you tell me my God isn't able! Here is the even cooler part. I didn't even ask for this, He just did it for me. He healed me without me even asking Him to. The Lord spoke to me one night of Revival and encouraged me that I would no longer need my medication. I believe the Lord just wanted to bless and show me more of who He is and that He would do it just because He could. There is nothing that Jesus cannot do. What is needed, is getting this revelation within us, and then living it out.

What do you need from Him today? What miracles are you contending for and believing for? Can I encourage you to not quit even when you feel like your prayers are hitting the ceiling? There were many times I didn't know if the Lord was even hearing my cry. There were times I felt like quitting because I felt I wasn't seeing any results and felt I was wasting my time. There were many times, I felt I was all alone in my pursuit of Revival Fire falling upon us and that it wasn't important to anyone else. But He is faithful, and He does hear His children. He will keep His promises,

He will deliver and come through, and it will always be right on time, every time. I am a living testimony. I, along with all these others you have heard from. So, believe and remember, we walk by faith and not by sight. <u>(2 Corinthians 5:7)</u>

**Now faith is the substance of things hoped for, the evidence of things not seen. <u>Hebrews 11:1 NKJV</u>.** Don't quit your faith, just because you aren't seeing results yet. Keep contending.

**DON'T QUIT YOUR FAITH, JUST BECAUSE YOU AREN'T SEEING RESULTS YET. KEEP CONTENDING.**

# Chapter 6

# Lasting Fruit

Numbers are great, but lasting results are so much better! Can I get an amen? What do I mean by that statement? We have all been tempted to take something we are involved in, appear to look appealing to the public eye. The thing is, if we must put a shell around something that really isn't authentic, then all it is, is hollow. I don't know about you, but I want something of consistency and real, not just a hollow shell.

I can remember starting out in youth ministry over 20 years ago. Whenever there would be talk about other youth groups or if you ran into someone you knew who was a youth leader or pastor, the conversation would always end up revolving around this statement; "So how many people are you running?" I had several of these conversations and even found myself playing the game. What I mean is, I would find myself in competition with other leaders trying to sound like we had it all together. That we were running these great numbers and had all these kids who were hungry for Jesus. We were the place to be! Is this relating to anyone else? Come on! I guarantee we have all been here a time or two, three or four and so on. It's like a fishermen story. I have fishermen in my home, so I have heard plenty of them, stories of a great catch being so large, and it was only just a guppy. We can all pause and laugh for a moment. But in all honesty, this becomes youth pastor stories, and I was stuck right in the middle of it.

In my mind when these conversations were taking place, I would even tell myself ahead of time, "Do not get caught up in the numbers, do not make this a competition!" But I kept falling in the trap.

In 2009, I had the amazing privilege of attending a youth leaders training located in Atlanta, Georgia led by Jeanne Mayo. She was known, at the time, as the leading youth pastor in America. I had the opportunity to attend this training for two years. I would drive down to Atlanta, and we would meet in Jeanne's home. It was a combination of youth pastors and leaders from all over the United States. I still consider this to be an amazing opportunity the Lord allowed me to experience. I am forever grateful for it, and I am still connected to many of those leaders today. In the home meetings, I began to see a group of people who became like family. We were all leaders, and we were excited about Jesus, with a desire to learn. The Lord began to show me there was more to leading than just talking about the numbers of your youth group. That was not my focus, it just seemed that numbers were all anyone spoke of rather than Jesus being the true focus. **I was fed up with all of that!** I was hungry to know more and had a desire to lead well. There was not a lot of strategy in place to know how to do it right. I got to see and hear from the hearts of people who were struggling just like I was, how hard it really was, and that no one had it all figured out. My focus began to shift, and the Lord began to get my perspective in a place of making disciples rather than growing a youth group. He began to show me that creating family was where it was at. I want to point out, that everyone that knew Jeanne Mayo and worked close to her called her mom. That is how she was known and what she was known for, a spiritual mother to a generation. All the leaders learned quickly to call her mom as well. She was centered around creating family and I believe this is the heart of Jesus. He desires for us to be in His family.

*But as many as received Him, to them He gave the right to become children of God, to those who believe in His name.*

<u>*John 1:12 NKJV*</u>

I confess, I did not have youth pastoring all figured out and, I still don't have all the answers. But praise Jesus, I am further than when I started. My passion for creating family and truly being a spiritual mother to a generation burns within my heart now, more than ever. I believe this experience and training helped attribute to this passion.

Now, fast forward a few years to when ETO was birthed in 2014. The Lord birthed a passion within me for a generation. I was sick and tired of the same ole routine and desired for real encounter with the Jesus I read of in the scriptures. I wanted a generation to burn for the things of God and become completely sold out to Him. I began to seek bigger than just my church. I wanted something in our state of WV for a generation to have of their own. I can remember daydreaming of having gatherings in the Summersville Armory and people coming from all over to gather and have encounters with Jesus and leave completely transformed.

It began with a vision. I remember, like it was yesterday, when I presented it to my pastor and he jumped on board and said, "Let's go for it." So, the preparations began. It began with much prayer and seeking direction on what the steps would be to begin to put things in place. I began reaching out for help with worship and it was as if the Lord was throwing crumbs my way leading me the whole time. He would connect me with people or highlight them to me and then confirm it. The vision was birthed in 2014 and our first ETO kicked off in July of 2015. This was set to be an annual conference. I sent letters out to all the surrounding churches inviting them to come and join us. I even went door to door and placed them at the doors of the churches. I did this also in the surrounding counties. The first year had a great start. We had people saved, rededicated, and filled with the Holy Spirit. However, it was nowhere near what I had seen in my heart. In all honesty, I was somewhat discouraged. I wanted to see us coming together and fighting for this generation. We were trying to get something off the ground and fight for our state. I wasn't looking to build our church, or my name, or for it to be about one place. I just wanted Jesus and this generation to want Him too. I have learned that people are very territorial and protective of what they have. Many don't want to combine or even cross denominational lines, because people are worried of sheep stealing or stepping on toes. My heart is grieved because we have gotten so closed minded, that we miss the entire purpose of the Gospel. We maintain within our four walls and are unwilling to think outside that box. We are "THE CHURCH," the "UNIVERSAL CHURCH." We should all be fighting for the same thing and learn to be unified in that. Winning people to Jesus, making disciples, and teaching them to do as Jesus did. The problem is we don't know how to come together because we have been taught to not like the church down the road because they do not believe like us. **This is wrong!**

I understand we each have a church to help, to grow, and contend for, but when we become so inward focused, then we are defeating the very purpose the church is here for. I had become that way to some degree and I wanted it broken off of me. I have always had an evangelistic draw to me and desired to move outside the four walls of a building.

<u>Think about this:</u> What if Jesus would not have allowed the ministry to the Gentiles or to the Samaritan woman?

What if "The Gospel" would have only been contained to the Jews? Where would we be?

Over each year I would see ETO growing, but it still wasn't where I knew we needed to be. There weren't a lot of outside churches that joined with us for the first couple years. I just could not get my point across, that I didn't want to steal anyone's young people. I just wanted to see a move of God and wondered if anyone else had the same desire. I wanted to see people running to the altar by the multitudes. My heart was to gather leaders together and to fight for a cause, fight for the Kingdom, fight for a lost and dying generation of young people. I needed something to break those walls down. I needed breakthrough! As each year passed, I began to see some growth taking place as I would gather people to be apart from outside the four walls. I didn't want people within our church only doing things. I wanted people outside our church to come and be a part. Our church was just a building to use. Still, we couldn't get past that territorial spirit where people wanted the credit. This is sad, but true. I questioned would we get to a place where we were just the vessel and Jesus, Him alone, was the One who receives all the Glory, not man? We must get this in our spirit as we desire for Revival in these last days. This isn't about our titles, positions, or leadership. **It is all about Jesus and Him alone!** We must get on His agenda and only do what the Father desires.

## IT IS ALL ABOUT JESUS AND HIM ALONE! WE MUST GET ON HIS AGENDA AND ONLY DO WHAT THE FATHER DESIRES.

Now let's fast forward to July of 2019 where everything changed. I remember talking with Nik about how this ETO felt different. I personally felt different about this year. I could not explain why. I'm not sure if my anticipation was higher than ever or if I was just desperate to see God do something. I knew it was different and I wanted all He had. Nik shared that he himself felt anticipation and felt something different and he had never even been to our church yet. I have shared and walked you through some specific nights of what took place, but I want to remind you, JESUS showed up! JESUS stepped right in and set a fire. He set a glory cloud over our county. He did do something different just as we had felt in the anticipation.

Short story: After revival broke out from the three-day conference, not long into it, I had a vacation scheduled with my family. I told my husband I wasn't going; I couldn't leave due to what I was seeing Jesus do. I struggled with going, all the way up to the day before leaving and knew I had to go with my family. If this REVIVAL was to continue, it was not contingent upon me, only the power of the HOLY SPIRIT! How selfish would I be to even think that!

**If this REVIVAL was to continue, it was not contingent upon me, only the power of the HOLY SPIRIT! How selfish would I be to even think that!**

I had to get past myself and allow Jesus to keep doing what only He could do. I remember praying throughout the revival, "Lord come do what only You can do." Sometimes, we must get out of the way for Him to do just that. This was part of me "removing my hands." Here I was again, having to obey His voice. It was hard for me to focus on vacation and relax. I would watch the Facebook lives every night and would be in contact every day with Nik and Pastor to keep up with all that was happening. I will never forget, when we got back home, we were driving to the service that night, and I could not wait to get there. An amazing thing I mentioned briefly before, is as Revival broke out from the three-day conference, other churches got involved. We had to move the revival to a gym that was owned by a church down the road from us. It belonged to New Life Assembly of God and the gym belonged to their Christian School. The Lord was bringing pastors together and churches together from all different denominations. We had Baptist, Non-denominational, Assemblies of God, Church of God, and Pentecostal Holiness all under one roof and who knows how many others. We all just wanted to see Jesus move.

I was so excited! I remember as my kids and I were heading back after vacation we began crossing into Nicholas County, West Virginia from Fayette County, West Virginia. It's hard to explain, but a wave hit me suddenly. I was taken back by it as I was trying to drive my vehicle. I remember looking at my daughter in the passenger seat and saying, "Do you feel that? It's like a glory cloud we just drove into." Some may say, "That is just your emotions." My emotions were involved, I will admit, but I also knew a weighty presence smacked me in the face and at that moment, I realized Jesus was nowhere near close to being done with Summersville. Again, what began as a three-day conference turned into ten straight weeks of real revival, real encounters, real salvations, real deliverances, real healings, and real freedom. All together; I was told there were around 350-400 salvations that came forth and between 450-500 people were filled with the Baptism of the Holy Spirit. I do not have an exact count on all the healings that took place, but there were so many. Some I have had the privilege of sharing with you.

I know this is not a Brownsville Revival or Cane Ridge Revival, from years past. However, there was no denying at this Summersville Outpouring Revival, Jesus was saving, setting free and making people whole in our little city. This was not a hype fest! We are over four years later; and we are still seeing the lasting fruit from this revival. I am personally connected with people and families who were a part of these numbers. They are still on fire, still serving the Lord, and now walking in their purposes and callings the Lord has placed upon them. That my friend is lasting fruit and worth it all.

Can you recall that moment you gave yourself completely to the Lord? Are you a part of His lasting fruit?

150

# Chapter 7

# MAINTAINING THE FIRE

How do you maintain what the Lord has given? This is a great question. King Jesus showed up over our county and rested a cloud of fire for a ten-week season. We got the privilege of experiencing His glory, wave after wave. It was only a small taste of what Jesus is yet to do, and what I have seen Him do since then. I believe there are waves of revival still yet to blow through our area and all over this state of West Virginia. The question is, how do we maintain what the Lord releases and continues to release?

I believe we must be careful of all the little foxes that try and come in and spoil the vine.

**"Catch the foxes for us,**

**The little foxes that are ruining the vineyards,**

**While our vineyards are in blossom."**

**<u>Song of Solomon 2:15 NASB</u>**

Our focus must remain upon the Beloved and Him alone. The moment we get our focus off Him it becomes focused on everyone else, and jealousy and competition can creep in and begin to spoil the root. Just look at the Israelites for example. After the Lord answered their cries and Moses led them out of Egypt, they turned around and began to complain, then they built an idol and began worshiping it because they didn't understand how to contend or tarry and wait upon the Lord. This is a problem with maintaining the fire. We do not know how to truly wait upon the Lord and be about His agenda rather than our own. We do things that feel good at the time and what may attract a crowd rather than seeking His very desire and will for what He wants in that moment.

We must be aware of these things in our own life, our own walk, and in maintaining the fire of Revival. We must remain revived, so revival becomes our innermost being and springs forth (from our bellies) into others. We must contend for the wells of Revival and the Fire to remain fanned. Many times, we get in a routine in the fight for revival and the contending for the fire. We must desire fresh bread and fresh manna daily. We need fresh Rhema from the very revelation of God and to daily pick up our cross and follow after all He is requiring. He requires obedience in our lives no matter the cost.

I began to see jealousy and competition creep in and try to choke out the fire the Lord had ignited and set upon the area. That is what can happen if we aren't careful and if man gets in the way of the move of the Lord, when man begins to put his hands on what only the Lord should have charge of. This is the thing that chokes out the flames of revival and then all you begin to see is smoke filling up the place.

Revival is messy! Revival busts up all that we know as church. That may not sound very encouraging, but it is still true. Revival comes in and tears down religious ideas and mindsets. It is in your face. It confronts every motive, idea, and thought. The goal is to clean all the junk out. We go through our day-to-day church life and forget about living a life of repentance and holiness. Jesus is looking for those with clean hands and a pure heart.

*Who may ascend onto the hill of the Lord?*

*And who may stand in His holy place?*

*One who has clean hands and a pure heart,*

*Who has not lifted up his soul to deceit*

*And has not sworn deceitfully.*

*He will receive a blessing from the Lord*

*And righteousness from the God of his salvation.*

<u>*Psalm 24:3-5 NASB*</u>

The problem is when all the junk begins to rise to the surface, attitudes, opinions, and arrogance can begin to creep in. We can begin to look at man instead of keeping our eyes upon the Beloved. The goal is to scrape all the impurities off so that our reflection becomes more like Jesus. What happens is we get all this junk on the surface and instead of scraping it off, we begin to throw it at one another. Refining is a process, its nasty, and its messy, yet it is vital to the disciple's growth and the church's growth.

*"But who can endure the day of His coming? And who can stand when He appears? For He is like a refiner's fire, and like launderer's soap. And He will sit as a smelter and purifier of silver, and He will purify the sons of Levi and refine them like gold and silver, so that they may present to the Lord offerings in righteousness.*

*Malachi 3:2-3 NASB*

I believe this is another picture of my dream which is an image of revival; the birthing of what the Lord desires, the refining to take place in purifying the gold, and the soap washing out the eyes of the babies.

Revival brings a refiner's fire into the house to clean out all the mess. The problem can be we don't allow the full process to take place, because it is not comfortable. It is painful, but it produces something so much more valuable. We need revival and we need to see it through to the very end, so that on the other side, we look more like Jesus and reflect the Bride, the radiant church He is coming back for. The Bride without spot or wrinkle. Revival irons out the wrinkles and removes the blemishes that must go. It removes agendas by man and puts us back in alignment with the King and with the Word of God. It requires us to make disciples and raise up sons and daughters as <u>Joel 2</u> and <u>Acts 2</u> talks about. It calls out the Spiritual mothers and fathers to wake up and begin helping this generation, so they don't fizzle out.

We must have the older men and women of God willing to walk with the younger generation to provide the wisdom and guidance they need. We must not damper the very zeal that is ignited within a young generation. The older generation needs this zeal and passion again, and the younger generation needs the wisdom and counsel. If we want to maintain the fire, then quit throwing water on the fire we have prayed for. When it becomes a little uncomfortable, we start to water down the flame and before long it burns out. Then, we wonder why no one wants to come back. We must learn how to maintain this fire and keep adding the wood. We must let the wind blow and increase the flame instead of throwing water and putting out the very fire the Lord answered with. He is the God who answers by fire.

***Then at the time of the offering of the evening sacrifice, Elijah the prophet approached and said, "Lord, God of Abraham, Isaac, and Israel, today let it be known that You are God in Israel and that I am Your servant, and that I have done all these things at Your word. Answer me, Lord, answer me, so that this people may know that You, Lord, are God, and that You have turned their heart***

*back." Then the fire of the Lord fell and consumed the burnt offering and the wood, and the stones and the dust; and it licked up the water that was in the trench.*

<u>*1 Kings 18:36-38 NASB*</u>

If you read the entire chapter of <u>1 Kings 18</u>, you will read of how the prophets of Baal were calling out to their gods to answer them in the way that they wanted. This may sound harsh, but I think, if we are not careful, we can become like the prophets of Baal. We have a set way of doing things with our rituals, our agendas, and then we pray and want God to answer how we want Him to answer. We have set up a god in our mind to fit our comfort, our need, and to become our little genie in a bottle type god. How dare us! This is a scary thought for me. I don't want to be like that. The Bible is clear when it says,

*"For My thoughts are not your thoughts,*

*Nor are your ways My ways," declares the Lord.*

*"For as the heavens are higher than the earth,*

*So are My ways higher than your ways*

*And My thoughts than your thoughts.*

<u>*Isaiah 55:8-9 NASB*</u>

Our problem is we want our thoughts to be His thoughts and our ways His ways. It doesn't work that way. He is Lord and we are not, He is the Creator, and we are the created. He is the only One who is worthy of all the praise, and we are the ones to adore and praise Him. When we can keep this mindset and heart posture, we just may aid in maintaining the fire we so long for.

If we are going to call on our God, the only God who answers by fire, then when the fires of revival hit our land let's not run away but run to. We cannot hide in a cave because we become too uncomfortable or don't like the fight that it stirs up. Let's prepare for the Elisha's who the Lord desires to raise up and give a double portion to. That is maintaining the fire and passing it on from generation to generation.

**LET'S PREPARE FOR THE ELISHA'S WHO THE LORD DESIRES TO RAISE UP AND GIVE A DOUBLE PORTION TO.**

## Chapter 8

# WHEN IT DOESN'T LOOK LIKE WHAT YOU THOUGHT

As I said before, REVIVAL IS MESSY! When revival comes and the confrontation happens, I believe it requires complete obedience to Jesus. This, my friend, is not always easy to walk out.

I am speaking from experience and not just attempting to write a bunch of pretty words on a page. I had to walk this in my own life. When the revival broke out in our church and went for ten weeks, the Lord had already been dealing with me personally on things in my walk. He had been showing me things in the Spirit for a few years prior. I knew something was transitioning in me, but I just wasn't sure what it would look like. At the time I served in quite a few positions within our church. Church administrator was one of them along with being a part of the worship team and young adult pastor. I knew the Lord was dealing with me about stepping away and had been for some time, even before revival had sparked. During the revival I was feeling even more pressed to transition into another place. I knew the Lord was orchestrating something bigger than I could wrap my head around and had been bringing the pieces together.

I must admit, I have grown to dislike the word, "transition." Reason being, it is costly, it comes with hard decisions, it comes with opposition, it requires obedience, it is uncomfortable and most of the time many will not understand it. What I have come to find out and learn over the years by walking through many of them; transitions are necessary to move you into the places the Lord orchestrates for you and for His purpose to come forth, that you may fulfill the assignment He desires in your life.

This most recent transition the Lord was requiring of me, I wrestled with the most. I shared with you earlier about being the youth pastor for 18 years. I had been discipled in this church and learned everything I knew up to this point. My pastor supported me in everything I put my hands to, and this was my family. I held many positions within this church, I had trust from the pastor and the leadership I felt I had earned over the years. I took what I did very seriously and wholeheartedly. I tried to be faithful in all I attempted to do and rarely missed any services. Many times, I was the first there and the last to leave. I was very careful when I said something was or wasn't of the Lord. My desire was to always have confirmation because I always wanted to represent Jesus well.  I knew in all this; **Jesus was asking something more of me.**  Why would the Lord ask more than what I was already doing?  You must understand; He wasn't asking me to add more to my plate, He was asking for everything I had on my plate.  He was asking me for EVERYTHING!  What I am getting at is… The Lord was saying to me, "I want all your positions!"

### "I want all your positions!"

He wanted it all!  All my titles, all my efforts, all my agenda, all my way of doing things, all that I had known and worked towards for 20 years.  I was wrestling with the Lord just like Jacob wrestled.  At least that is what it felt like.

*Then Jacob was left alone, and a man wrestled with him until daybreak. When the man saw that he had not prevailed against him, he touched the socket of Jacob's hip; and the socket of Jacob's hip was dislocated while he wrestled with him. Then he said, "Let me go, for the dawn is breaking." But he said, "I will not let you go unless you bless me." So he said to him, "What is your name?" And he said, "Jacob." Then he said, "Your name shall no longer be Jacob, but Israel; for you have contended with God and with men, and have prevailed." And Jacob asked him and said, "Please tell me your name." But he said, "Why is it that you ask my name?" And he blessed him there. So Jacob named the place Peniel, for he said, "I have seen God face to face, yet my life has been spared."*

<u>*Genesis 32:24-30 NASB*</u>

## HE WAS CHANGING MY NAME

I knew everything was about to change and that the Lord was about to change everything about me. **He was changing my name**! I wasn't going to be known as a title or position any longer. He just wanted my obedience as His child, and I was about to walk through a season of learning exactly what that entailed. I had to break out of the box I had been in for so long. The box I had learned to operate in, but the Lord was asking me to expand my view, my thinking, and my way of doing things. He was about to teach me how to operate in a whole new way, according to His will, and He was placing me in my new assignment. Understand that what I had been doing up to this point was not in any way useless or wrong. Over time I realized all those years were training and preparation for the season He was bringing me into. We never stop training in this walk as disciples. A disciple is ever learning, always growing, and should continuously be making other disciples. This is a bold statement, but I believe the moment you think you have arrived; I believe you are of no use to the King or His Kingdom because pride has set in, and you are about to fall. Remain teachable!

## REMAIN TEACHABLE!

I knew in my wrestling, just as Jacob; I was not going to let go until I knew I would get my blessing. I remember the night I sat down and met with the pastor and the leaders about stepping away. I knew the Lord had confirmed for me several times I was doing the right thing, and I was at peace, but the wrestling was still happening within me. My fear was letting people down that I loved so dearly. Yet, I knew I had to make this step.

I will never forget that night as the leaders and the pastor laid hands on me and prayed over me to commission and send me. Words were specifically said to me by the pastor, that I had his blessing. I felt the Lord give me such peace in that statement and the peace I felt afterward helped settle me even more. I know it wasn't easy and not everyone would agree. It was hard and uncomfortable, and I felt I let people down, but I do believe the Lord was in it all.

A few years before all this, I specifically remember driving to the church to work for the day and I was in prayer. I was crying out to the Lord and was in deep intercession and telling the Lord to "send me," whatever it took, just send me and I was willing to go. I can remember exactly where I was, in my drive, when I distinctly heard the Lord speak to me in what I felt was almost an audible voice. He said to me, "It will cost you." I took a deep breath and even went to speak back and said, "Lord, I know it is a cost," and He said it again but with more sternness, "No, it will cost you!" I began to weep at the realization of the seriousness of His voice and the response overwhelmed me. The Lord over the years has brought me back to this encounter but it was extremely highlighted during this season of Revival in my walk with Him. I believed the Lord was about to show me just what He meant by those words.

Can you imagine what it must have been like when the Lord told Abraham to pack up and go? To leave all that he knew and still not knowing where he would be going?

*Now the LORD said to Abram, "Go forth from your country, And from your relatives And from your father's house, To the land which I will show you;*

### *<u>Genesis 12:1 NASB</u>*

We must realize that our assignments are so much bigger than us. If you know anything about scripture, Abraham was being called away from what he knew all his life. It was not because the Lord was being mean, wanted him alone, or just for the fun of it. NO! It was for much greater purpose; it was for many generations to come. It was for you and for me. God had us on His mind even then. Think on that a moment, the Lord promised Abraham that he would be the father of many nations, and we have the privilege of being grafted into this promise. Thank you, Jesus! Notice, just a few chapters later in <u>Genesis 17</u>, the Lord changed Abram's name to Abraham. How could Abraham fulfill what the Lord said unless he was willing to be obedient to the leading of the Lord's voice and be willing to go through a name change. Be willing to "count the cost."


**Be willing to "count the cost."**

Now this brings me back to my dream. This is where the third part comes in to play.

### *Dream part 3*

*In the third part of this dream, I was in a house and was surrounded by my family. My sister, my uncle, who is an actual pastor, and my aunt. I knew it was all my family. They were trying to speak to me and change my mind in the dream and while this was happening, my phone was ringing, and it was my dad calling me. I woke up before answering the phone.*

### *Meaning:*

*Now I believe the meaning of this dream is this. My family within the dream represented my church family, sisters and brothers and aunts and uncles. People you become very close to. None of them wanted me to leave or step away and they were trying to convince me not to. My phone ringing and my dad calling I believe, represented my Heavenly Father calling me to answer Him.*

I want to be clear. In this dream my family wasn't bad for trying to convince me. It was that the Lord was requiring me to follow Him, His leading, and to answer His call; even when those you love, or those you are the closest to, do not completely understand at the moment.

During the revival, the Lord was putting pieces together for me like a puzzle. He was connecting me to specific people. My heart bore witness with them and all they were running after. Reason being, it was my heart as well.

The Lord has brought a lot of the pieces together over the last few years and continues to do so, as this has all played out. I continue to walk by the leading of the Lord. I can look back and see that nothing was like what I thought it would be, it was so much better. None of it has been easy to walk out, but it has been worth it all. I have gotten to see hundreds of salvations, healings, and deliverances, not just from this revival but from multiple others I have had the privilege to be a part of. If I had not stepped out and answered the call to what the Lord was asking of me, I would not be where I am today.

Can you see little pieces of the puzzle laid out for your life? You may not understand it all and you may not even like all that you see before you. I promise you this, Jesus has a plan, a purpose, and an assignment for you to fulfill. You just must be willing and obedient. Now these are easy words to type out, but they are hard words to live by and implement in our lives. I haven't done everything well. It took some wrestling on my part, but I know this, Jesus is Who I am after. I am not after fame or glory, or my name in the lights. I am pursuing King Jesus, His heart, and to please Him and Him alone. At the end of the journey, knowing Jesus and following Him is all that will matter. The Lord asked me for all my positions and my willingness to follow Him wholeheartedly. When I handed them to Him, I gained so much more; I gained the place at His feet. Whatever He asks of me, I will do, because Jesus received my yes, a long time ago.

What is the King asking of you today? What is the cost to see revival come to you personally and then to those around you? The mission is so much greater than us; it is to make disciples and, to see all come to Jesus.

*Go, therefore, and make disciples of all the nations, baptizing them in the name of the Father and the Son and the Holy Spirit, teaching them to follow all that I commanded you; and behold, I am with you always, to the end of the age."*

*Matthew 28:19-20 NASB*

Let us become "History Makers." History is vital to this generation to succeed now! I am not saying we live in history and do things that were done in history, but it is important to look back at history so that the same mistakes are not made. The lessons learned cause us to gain wisdom. What worked and what didn't! I believe this is the reason the story of the Summersville Outpouring needed to be recorded. This was a turning point for our city, for our county, and for our churches. It was much bigger than that, now that we reflect upon it. Revival came, messed up our ways of doing things, and took us to the foundation to build the exact way Jesus intended. There are lessons to learn from it, and epic moments to cherish. This revival is not to be forgotten but remembered and recorded.

Our entire nation was founded upon history, and we have a government that wants to rid the history of our forefathers! Let us not be that way! Why do you think Jesus said, "Do this in Remembrance of Me"? (1

Corinthians 11:24) He was speaking of communion and to do it remembering all He had done and sacrificed for you and for me. Do not cast aside history, I believe it is vital for growth and wisdom. Most of the kings in the Old Testament failed to do this, lost their way, and led generations away from the Lord. Those who chose to remember their fathers before them and devote their hearts to serving Jesus, had victory, and passed on Truth to a generation.

Let us remember what Our Father did! He gave His only begotten Son! (John 3:16) Learn and grow and don't repeat the same mistakes. What are we discarding and what are we holding on to?

Let us remember what Revival did, what it brought, how it changed us all, and the unity that was created. Let us keep burning and contending for revival that will turn the hearts of the people back to the face of Jesus. A place where we are willing to count the cost whatever He may ask or require from us. Let us continue to intercede and pay attention to those that the Lord may bring across our path, to run with, in order to see the Kingdom advance. It is still about saving the lost, setting captives free, the broken healed and the oppressed delivered. We all have something to do, are we doing it? I heard Jay Morgan recently make a statement that I believe goes well here, **"Obedience is greater than sacrifice, even if obedience is sacrifice."**

**"Obedience is greater than sacrifice, even if obedience is sacrifice." -Jay Morgan**

We have a generation that needs the wisdom of the old, but we have the older that needs the zeal of the younger. This is about generations. What are we leaving behind?

Let us reflect and remember so that we may gain, and our walk reaches further to the next generations!

**The testimony of Jesus is the Spirit of prophecy!**

**<u>Revelations 19:10 NKJV</u>**

My hope and prayers are that you go now and make history by following after Jesus with all your heart, soul, mind, and strength. Fulfill your assignment and the great commission whatever that looks like for you. It will cost you something, but I promise it will be worth it, if it is His voice you are following.

Let us do our part and make history. My purpose in writing and documenting all of this is so that a piece of history will not be forgotten of the Summersville Outpouring. It was a marking for many in their lives and they are lasting fruit from what took place there. I am lasting fruit from this revival, and I cannot be silent in telling all that Jesus has done.

*"for we cannot stop speaking about what we have seen and heard."*

*Acts 4:20 NASB*

Let us keep speaking of all He has said and done so that many come into the Kingdom. This my friend is REVIVAL and is only a taste of what is to come. It just may not look like what you think. It will look much better!

*'The latter glory of this house will be greater than the former,' says the LORD of armies, 'and in this place I will give peace,'*

*declares the LORD of armies."*

*<u>Haggai 2:9 NASB</u>*

# CONCLUSION

I could not begin to tell this story, share my personal testimony, or the testimonies of many others, if it were not for the obedience and commitment others have made to King Jesus. I am so thankful for each person that played a part in seeing this revival come forth. I am blessed to know many intercessors that pressed in and contended and are continuing to contend for revival in our city, our state, and even the entire Appalachia area. They are the fans that keep the flame burning. Do not ever underestimate or take for granted a true intercessor. They are vital to the birthing of true authentic revival.

We must understand that we all have a part to play in this journey. We all have been gifted, called, and given assignments by the Lord. It is up to each of us to first, surrender to the Lordship of Jesus and then pursue Him and Him alone. This journey is not about the pursuit of position, promotion, or the popularity with man. Revival is laying down our agenda, our way of doing it, our man-made ideas, and traditions to then pick up the Cross and follow. We must be willing to follow wherever Holy Spirit wants to lead and direct. We can say we are ready for that, but when we say, "Lord we are desperate, come and do what only You can do," all I know is we better be ready to get self out of the way. Revival brings us back to life and gives us another chance. It is about making Jesus the center of all we are and all we know. It is about the Church becoming exactly what Jesus desires His Bride to be. He wants the spots and the wrinkles removed so He may present His Bride, holy, pure, and radiant. Revival is all about the pursuit of ONE MAN. Revival is about all attention being upon this ONE MAN, JESUS. I believe when we grab ahold of this concept, hold onto it, and we are not willing to trade Him for anything else, we can then say, "This is Revival!"

I am forever thankful to Nik Walker and his team that said yes and showed up the night of July 19, 2019. Their yes to Jesus birthed hundreds more yes's and have continued to do so, not only in little Summersville, West Virginia, but across the state of West Virginia. I am honored to have witnessed this up close and personal. I am thankful the Lord has allowed me to be a spiritual mother to this young man along with many others from his team. I have since then, witnessed over a thousand people surrender their lives to Jesus and get baptized. I have also witnessed and participated in the evidence of signs, wonders, and miracles. I will cherish this opportunity the Lord allowed me to see and be a part of. To see Nik and his team, along with my own children, and this generation fulfill their purpose and assignment and win thousands more to the Kingdom of Heaven is a great honor and joy.

I witnessed a young man, young in ministry, full of zeal, passion, on fire for Jesus, and committed to the Lord preach the gospel with a boldness needed in this day and hour as of John the Baptist. This, along with many others and their obedience, sparked the flame and burst forth the well that poured out within our city. I believe revival came. ETO, Expect the Outpouring was just that. It became the Summersville Outpouring and me, along with many other people, churches, our city, and our state will never be the same because of it. This is the day Jesus answered and I will keep the testimony.

**THIS IS THE DAY JESUS ANSWERED AND I WILL KEEP THE TESTIMONY**

*Commit your actions to the Lord,*

*and your plans will succeed.*

***Proverbs 16:3 NLT***

I promise if you do this, He will unlock the call, the gift, and begin to reveal those very assignments He has set aside for you. What part will you play in the end time revival? I believe we are about to see it in its fullness. This story is only a taste of what Jesus is about to do.

Let me share one last encouragement with you to prove, yet again, the faithfulness of God. Since this revival of 2019, not only have I witnessed thousands give their lives to Jesus and the evidence of signs, wonders, and miracles, but the Lord was gracious to allow me to witness and participate in a conference, established in 2023, here in the state of West Virginia. This conference was specifically for a generation of burning ones. This also was a personal prayer of mine since the birthing of ETO. **The Lord answered again!** The Lord really can do exceedingly, abundantly more than we ask or think according to the power that works within us. (Ephesians 3:20)

I witnessed an answer to prayer called "Firebrand Conference," be established and hosted by Nik Walker Ministries. There is NO WAY, you will ever convince me that Jesus doesn't have a plan from the very beginning, and that He is in all the details. He sets up, orchestrates, and aligns everything, **ALL FOR HIS GLORY**. I've seen too much, and I believe within my spirit, we are about to see much more. Get ready, another wave is about to break out!

**Get ready, another wave is about to break out!**

*But my life is worth nothing to me unless I use it for finishing the work assigned me by the Lord Jesus—the work of telling others the Good News about the wonderful grace of God.  Acts 20:24 NLT*

I will leave you with this final word that I believe the Lord spoke to me in the middle of revival.

*"I will do what I have said I will do. My Word does not return void. For it will go out across the land and draw hearts back to Me. For I am loving and kind and patient and longsuffering. Keep pressing in to all that I have for you. There are no limits to My goodness and My grace. I Am relentless and it is My desire that all would come into the Kingdom and that none shall perish, but have eternal life with Me. I pursue and run after those who have turned away, but the time is now to return to Me while My grace is available. Do not wait, do not hesitate. Come now, come now. For this is the cry of My heart. This is*

*My heartbeat to see you in your fullness. Be the Bride I have longed for."*

*-Jesus*

# **REFERENCE PAGE**

1. C. Williams, (personal communication, October 1, 2021)

2. K. Moore, (personal communication, October 5, 2021)

3. A. Moore, (personal communication, October 14, 2021)

4. L. Meadows, (personal communication, December 2, 2021)

5. M. and E. Fagan, (personal communication, November 26, 2021)

6. J. Morgan, (personal communication, November 7, 2021)

7. Deut. 6:10-11; Zech. 4:9-10; Hab. 2:2-3; Acts 2:15-21; Joel 2:28-32; Psalms 37:23

8. Isa. 43:19-21; Luke 2:15-20; Matt. 15:25-28; Ezek. 47:1-9; Eph. 3:18-19; Matt. 6:33; Heb. 12:1-2; Hag. 2:8; Matt. 4:17; Rev. 5:6-10

9. 2 Sam. 6; Eph. 3:20; Romans 8:28

10. Rev. 19:10; 1 Cor. 11:23-26; Acts 10:34-48; Romans 8:34; 2 Cor. 5:7; Hebrews 11:1

11. John 1:12

12. Song of Solomon 2:15; Psalms 24:3-5; Malachi 3:2-3; Joel 2; Acts 2; 1 Kings 18:36-38; Isa. 55:8-9

13. Gen. 32:22-30; Gen. 12:1; Gen. 17; Matt. 28:19-20; 1 Cor. 11:24; John 3:16; Rev. 19:10; Acts 4:20; Haggai 2:9

14. Prov. 16:3; Acts 20:24

End